The Versatile Manager: A Grid® Profile

Robert R. Blake
Jane S. Mouton

DOW JONES–IRWIN
Homewood, Illinois 60430

Table of Contents

Preface

The objectives of managerial leadership are to maximize productivity, to stimulate creative problem solving, and to promote morale and satisfaction. Few would reject these lofty objectives. The great debate among managers, however, is with respect to the question, "What is the best way to achieve these objectives when working with and through others?"

One side in this debate is embraced by those who maintain, "There is no one best way. How you seek these objectives depends entirely upon the situation and its unique properties. Therefore, you may maneuver or manipulate, compliment or ignore, confront or compromise, depending upon what you see as the most probable way of achieving such objectives as the above."

The other side contends that "There are sound principles of human behavior. When they are adhered to, productivity, creativity, high morale, and satisfaction are the result. When they are violated, the price paid is in lowered productivity or lowered creativity, with satisfaction or morale reduced, as those through whom production is to be achieved recognize that these principles are being disregarded or violated." Those who embrace this idea of adherence to principles of human behavior go on to say, "The strategy of managerial leadership is to seek to bring sound principles of behavior into daily use. How this is done tactically depends upon the situation.'' For example, in day-by-day dealings a manager relates differently to the new employee than to the old hand. One is given encouragement and support, and mistakes are accepted with empathic understanding. To the other, appreciation is shown and the maximum possible autonomy extended to encourage the use of personal initiative, with the manager increasing the complexity of work to maintain a challenge. How the manager relates to each employee depends upon individual situations, but the principles of human behavior that are applied remain constant: openness, candor, and mutual respect, with maximum autonomy given to the extent that the individual is capable of self-direction.

This book identifies principles of behavior that underlie organizational effectiveness and tells how to put them into daily use. Evidence from some twenty-two behavioral science disciplines leads toward the conclusion that putting these principles into daily use creates human conditions conducive to increased productivity, strengthens creative problem solving, heightens satisfaction and morale, and even improves mental and physical health.

Versatility refers to the capacity of a manager to solve a large range of production/people. dilemmas in a sound way. Without such versatility, a manager may back off and leave problems unsolved or move in with pressure that will solve the immediate problem but create even larger ones. Or an evolutionary approach may be adopted, which allows other important problems to persist while focusing on one. These various courses of action are often pictured as the capacity to exercise flexibility because the manager shifts and adapts to the *limitations* inherent in the situation, severely restricting the organization in its pursuit of excellence. With such versatility a manager can apply sound principles of behavior in a way that will heighten effectiveness and contribute to the development of those with and through whom production is being accomplished.

History tells us that managerial leadership that degrades individuals results; in more unionization, increased government intervention, and oftentimes in the transfer of ownership out of the hands of individuals into those of the State. The outcome of this debate will determine the future character of business organizations, of industrial ownership, and of the role of government in exercising regulation and supervision.

ROBERT R. BLAKE

JANE SRYGLEY MOUTON

1
The Dilemma of Managerial Leadership

Day-by-day and week-by-week, often hour-by-hour, people are confronted with situations they have to manage. Invariably each of the situations is unique—it is something that has never happened before in quite the way it is happening now, and it is unlikely that it will ever happen in quite that way again. Even if its content in terms of material resources consists of the same items—money, materials, machines and equipment, land and buildings—it can be expected that some change, whether of quantity, availability, or quality, will occur. The people involved in it have had new and different experiences since the last occasion and they, too, have changed, even if they are the "same" people. Attitudes may be different, individual and group knowledge and skill may expand or improve, some lessons from past situations may be learned and remembered, others may have been forgotten or, maybe, never learned.

Each situation, then, is different. Some are different in simple, readily recognized ways while others are different in subtle or complex ways that are harder to identify and to understand, and often difficult to manage.

Every Situation Is Unique

Even in a given situation, each person involved is different. Each has his or her own values, different levels of knowledge and skill, different ways of contributing them, different sets of experiences, and, thus, different ways of looking at and evaluating the situation. Good leadership and direction of effort is needed if these variables and others that accompany them are to be managed effectively and according to principles that are sound. As far as people are concerned, the essence of good leadership is to treat each individual as a person in his or her own right, a person who is unique and who needs unique leadership to become committed to the needs every organization has for productivity and creativity. Commitment to these needs is lasting and trusting when it is generated in an environment that yields for each individual a high degree of personal satisfaction and freedom from stresses that become hazards to health. This is not to say that challenge and excellence are compromised but, rather, that each person feels, through the way he or she is led, directed, and managed, *drawn* to make a high level of contribution rather than *driven or compelled* to make it.

The issue then, indeed the whole point, is that the situation—be it of things or people—must make a difference. Everyone "knows" that and feels that it is right. Affairs have to be dealt with differently, according to the situation. All these thoughts meet the criterion of common sense for most of us. This is perhaps why schools of thought that advocate what has variously become known as "Flexibility," "Contingency," and "Situational Management" are appealing.

Flexibility, contingency, and situational management suggest that there are no principles to give guidance to managing different situations. This seems to be at variance with all forms of experience, in whatever field of human endeavor. Does one attempt to deny the principles of aerodynamics and the theory of flight because one is now making a paper dart for a child rather than the multiengined jet aircraft one might be responsible for designing during the working day? Does one alter the principles of sound nutrition when feeding a six-month-old infant instead of a mature adult? To do so would be to produce a paper dart that could not fly from one end of a room to the other and a child at risk of ill health and poor development. The key is that the principles of aerodynamics and the theory of flight are common to both the paper dart and the jet aircraft, but the *application* of them is different. This is also true for the feeding of infants and adults. The basic principle is that each needs protein, carbohydrates, vitamins, minerals, trace elements, and bulk as a basis for life. The application of the principle is, of course, different in each situation. Thus one sees the feeding bottle or maternal suckling for the infant and a two- or three-course meal of balanced content for the adult as totally different, yet they both represent the application of the same principles engineered to apply to different situations.

Just as these principles of aerodynamics and nutrition must be adhered to, if results are to be sound, so must the principles underlying effective managerial behavior be adhered to. One cannot and does not, in whatever walk of life, suddenly abandon principles because one is faced with a new situation—and, of course, *every* situation is new!

What, then, are the principles that underlie effective management? In this book, we set out those associated with superior performance of boss *and* subordinate, drawing on the work of researchers into more than twenty behavioral science disciplines. We offer an explanation of flexibility, contingency, and situational approaches to managing as a basis for comparing and contrasting them with a sound theory based on principles that are applied according to the needs of a situation.

Clearly, managers need to resolve the paradox that arises when differing variables in situations demand that the manager adapt to them without abandoning sound principles.

Here, then, is a dilemma. Should management spring totally from the needs of the situation, or should it be based on principles that give guidance for sound behavior? There is another way to say this. Should management be a series of tactics with no fundamental strategies based on consistent principles, or should strategies based on principles be used to give guidance and consistency so that the tactics can change, according to each particular situation?

Comparison of a Situational with a Versatile Approach

A dramatic illustration of this problem is related to exercising leadership with people of different levels of maturity. In what follows, maturity can be thought of with regard to a son or daughter, or it can be thought of with regard to a new employee versus an old hand.

Situationalism

The situationalist approach, involving as it does a series of rule-of-thumb tactics without underlying guidance from theory, prescribes a variety of tactics for dealing with a subordinate who is changing from immature to mature behavior. The immature person should be told what to do, and provided with no leeway or possibility of exercising self-direction until compliance with instructions has been achieved. When compliance has been realized, then the exercise of leadership becomes less controlling, with support and encouragement offered. Finally the person becomes mature and needs little or no guidance or supervision. Thus, the leader exercises an autocratic approach with an immature youngster or a new employee. After compliance has been given, the leader shifts to a selling strategy and when this is successful he or she may open the relationship up to participation. Finally when the youngster has reached maturity or the new employee has learned the ropes, the leader ceases exercising leadership except on a "check with me whenever you have a question" basis. This is rule-of-thumb situationalism. A technical appendix analyzing the limitation in specific situational approaches is provided in Chapter 14.

Versatility

The application of leadership based on behavioral science principles can be examined from a versatility perspective to see the opposition between these approaches.

A person exercising versatile leadership with an immature youngster or a new employee avoids interacting with that person on a "do as you are told" basis because, from a behavioral science perspective, it is known that people resist coercion, regardless of age or experience level. In comparison, we know that active participation in learning from one's experience is a sound basis of leadership for all maturity levels. Thus, the leader involves the youngster or the new employee in thinking through the situation or the task requirements and aids that person to develop insights into what is required to deal with the particular problem in a competent manner. As maturity increases, or as the new employee becomes more of an old hand, the character of exercising leadership changes because the situation confronting the youngster or person has, by now, changed. The other person now sees more, can test more alternatives, can see more broadly the implications of using one approach to solving a problem rather than another, and so on. Now the leader can further enrich participation through bringing new problems into the context of action to enable the other person to acquire "how to" skills on activities not previously a part of the situation.

The point is that the versatility approach recognizes the fundamental principle of participation as an important consideration in learning, in the development of responsibility, the ability to see consequences, and other areas.

The commitment to participation, from the standpoint of principles, remains constant. Participation continues to be experimental, open, conflict-focusing, and resolving. It permits the development of goals and objectives. The degree of leader participation in aiding the other person to learn from experience is tactical, depending upon the need for it.

Here, then, are two fundamentally different approaches to the exercise of leadership: the situational approach and the versatility approach. We can now explore the implications for mature leadership of the latter.

While a situation-determines-styles approach is appealing to conventional wisdom in an era when flexibility, adaptation, and reduced formality are accepted values, its consequences can be seen to be reduced organizational performance and lowered satisfaction for the individual.

Principles as the Basis of Action

The other side of the dilemma of how a manager might seek to develop personal effectiveness is *Versatility*. Versatility is present when an individual understands behavioral science principles and seeks to employ them in a consistent way as the basis for achieving productive results with and through other people. The versatility aspect is learning the skills necessary to apply the same principles under varying conditions, situations, or circumstances.

An important distinction being emphasized here is one that separates *strategy* from *tactics*. Strategy remains consistent with behavioral science principles. How strategy is applied in specific situations is tactical, however, depending on the circumstances themselves. Flexibility denies the existence of strategy; therefore tactics become all important, and reveal no underlying principles beyond the common-sense assumptions a manager may be guided by in attempting to deal with a given situation.

As an example, the versatile manager recognizes that the behavioral science principle of confronting differences in such a way as to learn their causes and eliminate them is the soundest way to resolve conflict. There are two reasons why this is so. One is that disagreements are relieved by insight. The other is that the tensions are relieved. Eliminating tensions arising from conflict in a situation means that energy remains available for dealing with production problems. Resolving tensions is mentally healthier than having to live with them. A versatile manager seeks to resolve conflict through confronting its causes and in managing in ways consistent with other principles of sound behavior.

Does this mean, then, that a versatile manager rigidly applies a principle without regard for the particulars of the situation to which it is applied? If not, what does it mean?

A versatile manager is concerned with applying a

given and a sound principle in an appropriate way. Thus, in dealing with a new employee, discrepancies in opinion that might lead to conflict are dealt with in a different manner than conflict that arises with an employee of longer-standing. With the newly hired subordinate, this manager might first examine the events leading to their differences. In this way causes of conflict can be identified that both boss and subordinate could otherwise fail to recognize. In contrast, the long-term employee understands quite well the activity being undertaken. It would be wasteful to engage in the same tracking needed with a new person. It is possible to reach the core of the difference more quickly and explore the causes of its origin. In both cases confrontation is relied upon as the basis for a meeting of minds. The principle remains constant but the application varies with the circumstances that confront the manager.

Viewed in this way, rejecting the principle that there is "one best way" to conduct human relationships is equivalent to rejecting the proposition that effective behavior is based on scientific principles. The view that principles of behavior underlie specific behavioral phenomena is consistent with views held about all other areas of scientific inquiry. We know that principles of physics underlie and explain a vast range of phenomena in inanimate nature. Principles of biology account for the phenomena of life and make them predictable. By analogy, principles of behavioral science should underlie effective management, providing guidelines for soundness of action and making events predictable.

When basic principles of the physical, biological, or behavioral sciences are disregarded, it can be expected that the resulting side effects and operational consequences will be damaging. Gravity is a constant physical principle, but it affects the engineering design of mechanisms used in space flights differently than it affects those used in undersea exploration. Biological principles of nutrition are constant, but the recommended diet for an infant of six months differs from that for a person forty years old. Biological principles governing the transfer of oxygen to the blood can be violated by an excessive smoker, but not without shortening the individual's expected life span. Managers who manage without attention to the basic principles of behavioral science will soon discover that their tactics are likely to lead to lowered morale, creativity, and job satisfaction in members of the work force, with resultant lowering of productivity and harm to the business as a whole.

Which Is the Sounder Way to Manage?

If this question were asked of any group of managers today, an almost even split between those favoring flexibility and those favoring versatility would probably result, with the majority view possibly falling on the flexibility or situational side. This is because it is seen to be "practical" in the context of common sense. Flexibility is an approach that gives people maximum freedom to deal with each circumstance as they see fit. It requires no detailed knowledge of the principles of human behavior. Rather, it relies primarily on intuition, ingenuity, sometimes on cunning.

By comparison, versatility is sound to the extent that the principles of behavior on which it is based can be stated in terms of how they affect productive and creative behavior. It is an approach that calls for systematic thinking and deliberate planning of appropriate action and for reliance on insight and understanding to deal with situations.

What little research there is that supports flexibility as a sound approach is limited in both depth and scope. On the other hand, there is much research to support the conclusion that versatility promotes productivity, creativity, satisfaction, and health. This research is evaluated later.[1]

Growth and development toward increased effectiveness by bosses, colleagues, and subordinates can be stunted or distorted by violating the behavioral science principles of participation, conflict resolution, goal setting, and so on. Even more dangerous are the possibilities of long-term damage to involvement, morale, and readiness to persevere in finding valid solutions to important problems with, finally, diminished productivity and profitability.

Just as basic principles of physics must be observed

to design an aircraft and basic principles of biology must be followed in an effort to increase longevity, so following the basic principles of behavioral science is the "one best way" to develop real and usable strength in boss-subordinate relationships. That way is to base decision making on scientific principles as verified by basic experimental work and applied with versatility to specific situations.

2
The Grid

Exercising power and authority is of overriding importance in managing, and there are good and bad ways of doing it. The first step in strengthening the exercise of power and authority is to learn the theories of the Grid. This learning will clarify the range of options available to a manager when he or she is searching for ways to exercise power and authority in the conduct of everyday business affairs. Having learned the grid theories, each manager is in a position to assess his or her leadership style and to see opportunities for change that can make for more effective leadership.

The Grid Dimensions

The Grid is based on three different dimensions or factors. The horizontal dimension is a concern for production. This means bringing about a result either directly or through subordinates. The vertical dimension is concern for people, for subordinates as human beings. The third dimension relates to one's own underlying motivations when the first two dimensions come together in various combinations.

Rather than trying to deal with these three dimensions all at once, we will examine the first two in this chapter

FIGURE 2.1

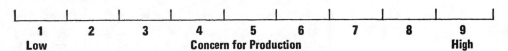

1	**2**	**3**	**4**	**5**	**6**	**7**	**8**	**9**
Low			**Concern for Production**					**High**

and the third in the next chapter. Then we can put them all together coherently.

FIGURE 2.2

The first (horizontal) dimension is *Concern for Production.* We know that this concern is not present in different people to the same degree and that it ranges through a scale. A boss is concerned with the production of things, a salesperson is concerned with achieving sales volume, and so on. Any outcome or result is a thing. In the same way that concern for production is not present among different people to the same degree, it is not necessarily present to the same degree for the same individual at different times. What we need, in other words, is to understand the meaning of degrees of concern.

Think of concern for production as a scale of degrees. This ranges from 1, a very low concern, to 9, a very high amount of concern, as illustrated in Figure 2.1.

The second (vertical) dimension is *Concern for People.* These are the people in our lives with and through whom we interact day in and day out. People can mean subordinates, customers, colleagues; whomever we relate with in going about our daily activities. Concern for people also varies through a number of degrees. Figure 2.2 shows degrees of concern as a nine-point scale, ranging from 1, a very low concern for people, to 9, a very high degree of concern.

How these concerns combine in a person reveals the manner in which that person thinks about achieving production through people, as shown in Figure 2.3. This represents a variety of possible theories for how to exercise power and authority.

The lower right corner of the Grid is seen in Figure 2.4. It is labeled 9,1 (referred to as "nine-one"). In this corner of the Grid a high concern for production (outcomes)

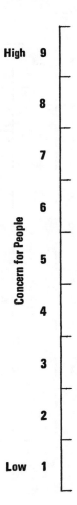

is combined with a low concern for the people with whom one is dealing. A manager with a 9,1 orientation concentrates on maximizing production by exercising power and authority unilaterally and exacting obedience from subordinates. We call a person who operates in this way a 9,1-oriented individual.

FIGURE 2.3

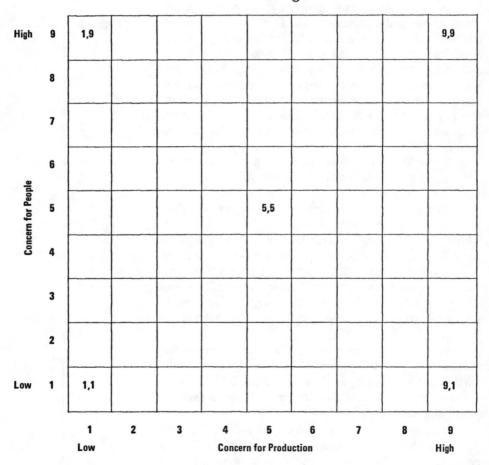

THE GRID®

FIGURE 2.4

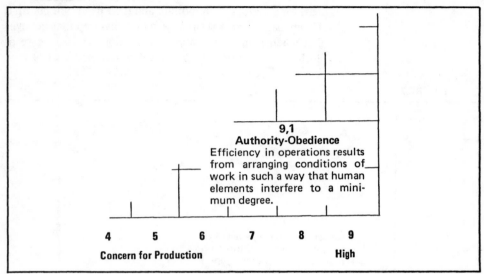

9,1
Authority-Obedience
Efficiency in operations results from arranging conditions of work in such a way that human elements interfere to a minimum degree.

| 4 | 5 | 6 | 7 | 8 | 9 |

Concern for Production   **High**

FIGURE 2.5

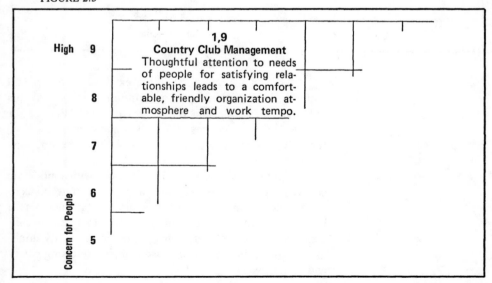

1,9
Country Club Management
Thoughtful attention to needs of people for satisfying relationships leads to a comfortable, friendly organization atmosphere and work tempo.

High   9

       8

       7

       6

Concern for People   5

A 1,9 orientation is shown in Figure 2.5, where concern for people is all-important and their needs are put first. The manager acting according to these assumptions believes that when people are happy, production will take care of itself without the need for close direction and control.

FIGURE 2.6

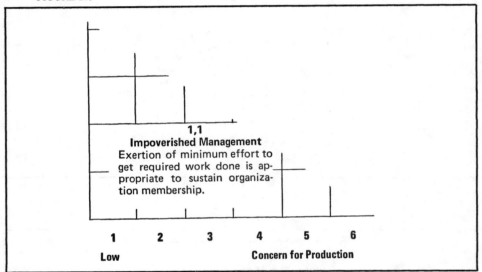

1,1
Impoverished Management
Exertion of minimum effort to get required work done is appropriate to sustain organization membership.

1   **2**   **3**   **4**   **5**   **6**
Low   **Concern for Production**

As seen in Figure 2.6, little exercise of power and authority is characteristic of a 1,1-oriented manager. This individual has little concern either for production or for people. He or she desires little (other than security), strives for little, gives little, gets little, and cares little, one way or the other.

Figure 2.7 shows the 5,5 orientation, with a moderate concern for production coupled with a moderate concern for people. A manager with this orientation maintains a balance between outcomes and people so that neither concern dominates the other, going along with majority thinking to avoid being seen as unreasonable in exercising power and authority.

FIGURE 2.7

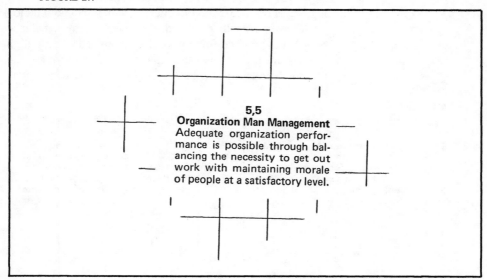

5,5
Organization Man Management
Adequate organization performance is possible through balancing the necessity to get out
work with maintaining morale
of people at a satisfactory level.

FIGURE 2.8

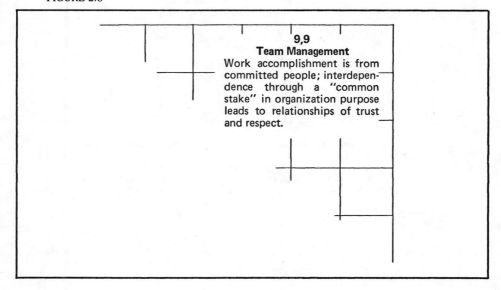

9,9
Team Management
Work accomplishment is from
committed people; interdependence through a "common
stake" in organization purpose
leads to relationships of trust
and respect.

The 9,9 orientation, seen in Figure 2.8, involves a high level of integration of concerns rather than domination of one over the other or a state of equilibrium or balance between them. The 9,9 approach demonstrates that a high concern for production can be pursued in ways that engage the involvement, participation, and commitment of subor-

FIGURE 2.9   THE GRID_®

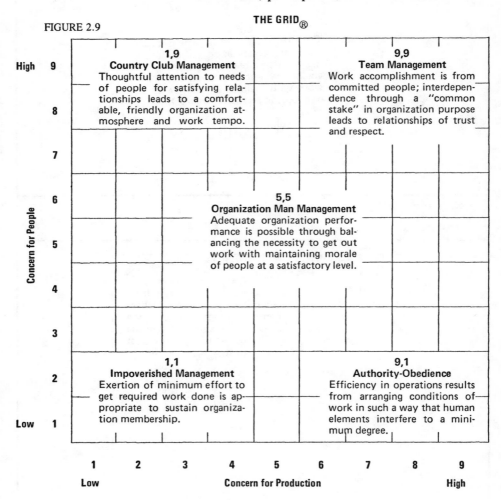

High   **9**   **1,9**
Country Club Management
Thoughtful attention to needs of people for satisfying relationships leads to a comfortable, friendly organization atmosphere and work tempo.

9,9
Team Management
Work accomplishment is from committed people; interdependence through a "common stake" in organization purpose leads to relationships of trust and respect.

6   **5,5**
Organization Man Management
Adequate organization performance is possible through balancing the necessity to get out work with maintaining morale of people at a satisfactory level.

Concern for People

1,1
Impoverished Management
Exertion of minimum effort to get required work done is appropriate to sustain organization membership.

9,1
Authority-Obedience
Efficiency in operations results from arranging conditions of work in such a way that human elements interfere to a minimum degree.

Low

1   2   3   4   5   6   7   8   9
Low   **Concern for Production**   **High**

dinates in achieving the highest possible standards in terms of quality, quantity, and personal satisfaction.

Many lines of evidence lead to the generalization that a 9,9 orientation is the soundest approach to managing production with and through people. The evidence comes from a variety of sources. Higher actual productivity, better stimulation and pickup of creativity, and increased job satisfaction are all brought about by employing a 9,9 approach to management.

A considerable challenge to development is opened up when it is acknowledged that the 9,9 approach constitutes the soundest way of managing. It thus becomes important to acquire the skills essential for dealing with the widest possible range of situations in a 9,9 manner.

A summary of the Grid theories as they relate to concern for production and concern for people is shown in Figure 2.9.

With this basic knowledge of Grid theories, we are now in a position to examine in a deeper manner what the 9,9 way of managing entails. The 9,9 orientation is the scientifically valid way of integrating the needs of people and their needs of production. It is based upon behavioral science principles, nine of which are of particular importance. Learning these principles and how to bring them into daily use constitutes the versatility aspect of the 9,9 way of managing. In a word, it is *versatility.*

Principles as the Basis of 9,9 Management

What behavioral science laws must be observed to ensure sound supervision? The following list is based on evidence from many applied behavioral science disciplines. The validity of these principles is supported by research in social psychology, sociology, anthropology, mental health, counseling, psychiatry, political science, history, and by field studies of business effectiveness. They are also validated in reverse by demonstrations of the negative behavior produced by their violation in the fields of criminology and penology, and by studies of the effect on people of colonialism, slavery, indentured servitude, and other forms of repression.

A background statement gives character to these principles. When they are brought into daily use, boss-subordinate interactions are characterized by mutual trust and respect. Trust and respect, in other words, are the end results of sound behavior. Sound behavior is also productive and creative in the operational sense. Other things being equal, productivity, creativity, personal satisfaction, and mental and physical health are best served when these principles are believed in and put into practice.

These principles, which prove productive, include the following.

- Fulfillment through contribution is the motivation that gives character to human activity and supports productivity.
- Open communication is essential for the exercise of self-responsibility.
- Conflicts are solved by direct confrontation of their causes, with understanding and agreement as the bases of cooperative effort.
- Being responsible for one's own actions is the highest level of maturity and is only possible through widespread delegation of power and authority.
- Shared participation in problem solving and decision making stimulates active involvement in productivity and creative thinking.
- Management is by objectives.
- Merit is the basis of reward.
- Learning from work experience is through critique.
- Norms and standards that regulate behavior and performance support personal and organization excellence.

These statements represent different facets of a 9,9-oriented management strategy. Each reflects in its own way the basic proposition that there is one best way to manage.

The principles cited above will be described in greater detail in the following pages.

Fulfillment through contribution is the motivation that gives character to human activity and supports productivity

Fulfillment through contribution means to be useful, to make a difference, to be productively helpful to others. When people are committed to the success of the larger organization of which they are a part, they are motivated to take the actions essential for its success. Fulfillment is derived from making such contributions. Like survival, the need to gain satisfaction from contributing seems to be a basic human motivation.

Open communication is essential for the exercise of self-responsibility

When communication is free and open, organization members have access to all information that is available and pertinent to their interests and responsibilities. Organization members can make maximum contributions only when the information requisite for sound thinking is available.

Conflicts are solved by direct confrontation, with understanding and agreement as the bases of cooperative effort

When people get together on a shared participation basis characterized by open communication, it is inevitable that differences will arise as to how to solve problems or which course of action to take. Eventually choices must be narrowed down and one selected from several. When conflict becomes intense, mutual trust and respect can be severely eroded, communication distorted, and feelings of personal responsibility substantially reduced.

Confrontation means taking a problem-solving approach to differences and identifying the underlying facts, logic, or emotions (prejudices, preconceptions, or antagonisms) that account for them. When conflicts are resolved through confronting and understanding the causes, people feel a responsibility for finding the best answer and exerting the necessary effort to do so.

When people participate openly in resolving conflict to find solutions to problems that require concerted action, decisions that result in understanding and agreement are possible. Understanding and agreement generate conviction and commitment to an outcome and stimulate the effort essential for realizing it.

Being responsible for one's own actions represents the highest level of maturity and is only possible through widespread delegation of power and authority

The ability to make a maximum contribution depends on the presence of the capacity to take initiative and exercise responsibility for one's own actions in a voluntary, spontaneous, and yet interdependent way. The fullest exercise of responsibility is possible only when authority for self-responsible action flows downward in the organization. In these circumstances opportunities to be more productive and creative can be acted on by those who see them.

Shared participation in problem solving for recommending decisions stimulates active involvement in productivity and creative thinking

Involvement means that people feel they have a stake in the outcome of a decision or an action. It leads to the notion that people will support what they help to create. Shared participation in problem solving stimulates involvement and results in the motivation to make a contribution.

Management is by objectives

Productivity and creativity are enhanced when individuals engage in achieving goals to which they are personally committed. Management-by-objectives is the operational way of gaining the benefits that are possible when individuals are goal-directed. What this means is that managers learn to identify the goals that are to be pursued and then set in motion the kinds of activites and efforts essential for achieving them. When personal commitment is attached to the goal, then one is drawn to it, seeks to achieve it, thinks about how to reach it, and makes the effort necessary to attain it. Behavior becomes purposeful and orderly. When management-by-objectives through goal setting is done in the proper manner and is based on openness, trust, and understanding, the personal goals of individuals and the goals of the organization tend to become integrated and harmonious.

Merit is the basis of reward

There are two criteria for evaluating individual contributions to the organization: (1) Does the contribution further the organization's prospects of success? (2) Will the contribution have no adverse side effects? This is the meaning of reward based on merit.

When reward is based on merit, organization members experience the system of promotion and pay as being just, fair, and equitable. The important issue is that only when reward acknowledges personal contribution is the effort to make contributions reinforced.

Learning from work experience is through critique

Critique is a process of stepping away from or interrupting an activity to study it to learn what is going on, to see alternative possibilities for improving performance, and to anticipate and avoid activities that will have adverse consequences.

Critique is a more or less "natural" way of reflecting on what is happening or what has happened. When organization members have widespread understanding of and skill in utilizing critique, it becomes possible to accelerate the rate of learning and in this way to advance progress much more rapidly than is possible when trial and error is the basic learning approach.

Norms and standards that regulate behavior and performance support personal and organization excellence

Much of our behavior is socially regulated by norms and standards to which each of us conforms. When norms and standards are set at high levels and when people are committed to them, they stimulate the pursuit of excellence and contribute to the satisfaction people derive from work.

Applying these nine principles of behavior to daily work helps ensure that human relationships will be based on mutual trust and respect. When they are violated, human trust and respect are diminished. An organization can maximize the involvement of its members in its success by putting these principles to daily use. Then it becomes possible to maximize the use of financial, technical, natural, and human resources, not only in pursuit of the organization's success but also in simultaneously promoting the satisfaction and health of organization members.

Strategy Versus Tactics of 9,9

Considered from a behavioral science point of view, these nine principles undergird sound behavior, just as certain principles of physics undergird sound engineering. Violate principles of physics in the engineering of a bridge or a building, for example, and you get disaster—the collapse of the structure. Violate the principles of sound behavior and invite similar disaster—collapse organization.

The idea of strategic use of a tactical approach can be viewed as analogous to nutrition. Nutritionally speaking, there is one best way of maintaining the body in a healthy condition. The strategy involves adhering to nutritional principles as they relate to the intake of protein, fat, carbohydrates, plus a number of minerals, vitamins, and so on. Not all of the details have been worked out, but the principles are well established: intake above an optimum may produce obesity; intake below the optimum may lead to fatigue, malnutrition, and susceptibility to diseases.

Thus, optimum intake is a principle of sound physical health. Disregard it and health troubles are imminent. However, the manner in which sound nutritional behavior is acquired is a tactical matter, contingent upon the availability of various foods. For instance, protein may be acquired from a number of sources. It makes no difference, from the standpoint of nutritional principles, what the particular source is, but protein simply must be acquired.

This is an example of the relationship between strategy—i.e., eating behavior calculated to satisfy nutritional principles—and the particular tactics through which these nutritional principles are met, varying with circumstance, availability of foods, and so on.

In the managerial context, a boss violates sound principles of behavior only at the price of sabotage, apathy, boredom, saluting, going along to get along, and other kinds of adverse reactions. When these principles are violated in the extreme, the result is heart attack, high blood pressure, migraine, asthma, ulcer, and other physical disorders. All of these are diseases of civilization essentially unknown in historical times, and even currently unknown in more primitive, preindustrial communities. They must, therefore, stem from the ways we manage ourselves and others.

The concept of versatility provides for understanding how leadership can consistently be based on sound principles of behavior and yet be brought into every day use in creative and constructive ways that are (1) able to strengthen profitability, (2) optimal to problem solving and productivity, (3) unlikely to generate negative side effects, (4) stimulating to growth and development toward maturity of those involved in the situation, and (5) unique to particular situations. The manager whose leadership is governed by behavioral science principles searches for ways of applying them that are tailored to each situation. The principles themselves are constant and unchanging. They define the strategy of a 9,9-oriented manager. Their engineering applications, or tactics, are specific to the work situations where employed. Thus principles are not violated and disregarded when the situation changes. What shifts are the tactics of application, which do vary, depending on the situation.

The issue of tactics under a 9,9 orientation is this. The specific approach, for example, when a boss is supervising a mature colleague is different from that when working with an immature beginner. The strategy of a 9,9-oriented effort to achieve production through the utilization of people remains constant, but the tactic in each case involves quite different on-site behavior and is contingent upon the situation.

Several examples demonstrate how principles have different applications, depending on the situational specifics. Take the behavioral science principle concerned with self-responsibility.

A sound boss-subordinate relationship is one that honors this principle. For instance, a manager is needed in another location, and a transfer appears to be the best solution. Is a person told "Go, or else . . . " or is subtle leverage applied? No, the subordinate is aided to see the costs and benefits for the company and the implications for his or her career, family, and friends of accepting the transfer rather than rejecting it. The decision is based on the subordinate's taking responsibility for his or her own actions with a full understanding and realization of the alternatives and the consequences of each.

Here is another example of the same principle applied to a different situation. The subordinate is a newcomer, a person without previous experience. Learning from critique is the basis of inducting the newcomer. The boss demonstrates and tells the subordinate what to do, encourages the individual to experiment and to learn from mistakes. The manager provides ample coaching and support as the newcomer gets acquainted with the job. They both critique the performance at the beginning of, during, and after work activities have been completed. The boss takes responsibility for assisting the subordinate to see angles, options, and alternatives. All along the line, this manager honors the individual's capacity to learn by creating a climate within which the subordinate can practice, experience, critique, ask for help, and control the pace of learning. Positive involvement accelerates the learning curve.

Behavioral science principles are honored in both cases but in different ways, depending on the particular situation to which they are applied. This is versatility. It demonstrates how the 9,9 leadership strategy can be the "one best way," with variations in how it is employed to fit varying situations.

One more example involving management-by-objectives will bring the issue clearly into focus. Once again, comparing a new recruit with an experienced employee will illustrate the difference between strategy and tactics.

From the standpoint of management-by-objectives, a boss would not sit down with a new recruit to discuss long-term career goals. The new employee is concerned only with tomorrow, next week, or this month. The goals are immediate and often narrow, by virtue of the new recruit's limited understanding of the situation, developing skills, and so on. Thus goals with a short-term perspective would be appropriate in the case of this individual.

The same issue is seen in an entirely different perspective for a long-term employee. Then the time frame for management-by-objectives may entail a lifelong career. The next fifteen or twenty years may be the period needed for attainment of realistic objectives in the situation facing this employee. The actual competencies of the person would be evaluated against objectives of this magnitude.

In the first case, it would be "bad" management to disregard the new recruit's inability to see the situation and to "force" a consideration of career-wide objectives. In the second case, it would be inappropriate to talk with a long-standing employee and keep the conversation limited to tomorrow, this week, or this month.

What has shifted in the two cases is not the strategy. The stategy is one of gaining involvement of the person in setting objectives toward which he or she can strive in a committed and orderly manner. What have changed are the tactics employed. In the first case the tactical issue is short-term; in the second, long-term. Management-by-objectives remains a constant in the situation. It is the manner of application that varies with the situation.

SUMMARY

Applying behavioral science principles to managing production with and through people results in relationships that are productive and creative and that are based on mutual trust and respect. These principles are related to motivation, responsibility, participation, communication, decision making, conflict solving, goal setting, financial and other rewards, and learning through critique.

Scientific principles find their way into daily use through engineering applications. We are familiar with the principles of physics in engineering but less familiar with behavioral science principles in management. The strategic level of thinking involves the principle. The utilization of that principle in a particular or unique situation is design-engineering or tactical. Thus a versatile manager is one who is able to manage according to behavioral science principles in such a way that the specific managerial actions taken are designed to fit the particular requirements of concrete situations.

Ensuing chapters explore the principles in detail and examine the problems of applying them in everyday situations.

3
Fulfillment Through Contribution

A significant part of our thoughts and feelings about production and people involves the question, "How are we motivated in life and work?" If excellence is our goal, our motivations may have to change in directions that will permit us to make our organizations into model institutions in which to live and work.

Personal motivations have never been well understood because, up to now, we have had no valid way of sorting them out and of comparing one set of motivations with another. Thus managers have found it difficult to develop strong convictions about what best motivates people to become involved in production. Yet only when means of motivating people are based on sound principles of behavior can we expect to work with and through others in ways that solve problems, create positive involvement, build morale, and make us healthier in mental and physical terms.

The Grid framework provides a basis for understanding personal motivations. With it we can answer the question, "What is the personal motivation of a manager who operates according to each Grid style?" This motivational dimension intersects the Grid at a right angle.

Figure 3.1 shows the motivational scale, which is different from the *Concern for Production* or *Concern for People* scales, both of which run from a low of 1 to a high of 9. This scale reveals our motivations as "bipolar." It is based on a continuum from a negative pole through a neutral zone to a positive pole, as seen in Figure 3.1.

FIGURE 3.1

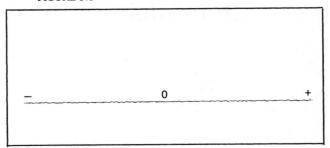

The plus (⁺) end tells what activities in life "pull" us, that is, what we strive to reach in our own views of ourselves. The minus (⁻) end is what we seek to avoid. There are five of these scales, one relating to each Grid style. We can now examine how they fit on the Grid.

FIGURE 3.2

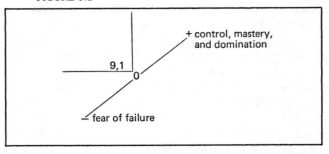

9,1　　The 9,1 motivational scale, as seen in Figure 3.2, intersects the Grid at a right angle to the other two. The zero, neutral, or middle point of the scale is located on the Grid at the point where the 9 of concern for outcomes meets the 1 of concern for people.

The plus end of the motivational scale—what a 9,1-oriented person strives for in life—is "control, mastery, and domination," indicating that a 9,1+-oriented person seeks to come out on top, using people as tools in the pursuit of production. The minus end is "fear of failure," demonstrating that for a 9,1--oriented person, defeat in getting the things desired is tantamount to accepting one's own weakness and personal inadequancy. Activities in between, around the zero point, are not important for proving oneself one way or the other.

Personal motivations of the kind found in the 9,1-oriented person influence a manager's involvement as well as the way in which his or her behavior influences subordinates. A person with a 9,1 managerial orientation is likely to be involved and committed to organization purposes. Such a manager is free to drive him or herself and others in the interest of results. Subordinates are viewed as little more than agents of production and are seen as being employed to do the dictates of the manager's will.

From the standpoint of subordinates, however, the effect on their involvement is likely to be quite different. Such managerial behavior is seen as thoughtless and arbitrary, giving subordinates a feeling of being "used." Along with this is the danger that a 9,1-oriented manager will stimulate antiorganization involvement where subordinates use slowdowns and other forms of work hindrances as a means of discharging resentment toward 9,1-oriented practices.

1,9

The motivational scale for a 1,9-oriented person is pictured in Figure 3.3.

In this Grid style a person's dominant plus motivation is to gain the warmth and approval of others. That is the consuming interest in life. To suffer rejection is what is most feared as the minus motivation. Rejection demonstrates to 1,9--oriented individuals that they are unworthy of acceptance.

The 1,9+-oriented manager sees "togetherness" as

FIGURE 3.3

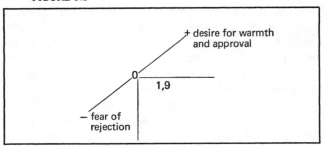

a way of getting approval through making subordinates feel a part of one big happy family. This manager goes all out to see that suboridinates are satisfied with working conditions to avoid being rejected by subordinates. Low concern for production and a high concern for acceptance help generate identification with the work group and enjoyment of its social activities, both on the job and beyond. Commitment is focused on the human dimension, with production or task accomplishment more or less eliminated. This occurs when high morale combines with low productivity.

1,1   The motivations that explain a 1,1-oriented person are pictured in Figure 3.4.

FIGURE 3.4

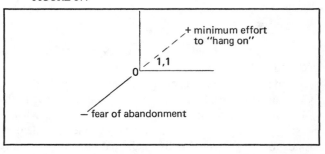

We see the plus motivation of a 1,1-oriented person as seeking to continue the activities he or she is currently engaged in by applying only the minimum effort. The minus pole is avoiding activities that might reveal that the 1,1-oriented person has become so uninterested that he or she will be asked to leave.

The involvement of subordinates managed by a 1,1-oriented manager is likely to be low because of the lack of leadership and enthusiasm of the boss, who is primarily interested in exerting no more than the minimum effort necessary to hang on. The exception is the eager subordinte who misinterprets the boss's indifference and accepts it as delegation, or, seeing it as indifference, seizes the "delegation" anyway.

A 5,5-oriented person's motivations are illustrated in **5,5** Figure 3.5.

FIGURE 3.5

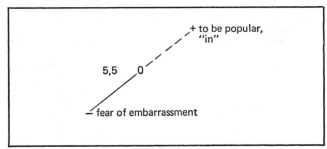

The plus end of the scale is a concern with doing whatever is necessary to be socially accepted and popular—an "in" person. Satisfaction is derived from status and prestige rewards within the system. The minus pole entails feelings of anxiety regarding the possibility of criticism, censure, or not "belonging." Criticism and censure signal loss of status through social demotion. That is what a 5,5-oriented person most dreads.

The 5,5-oriented manager attempts to gain acceptable results by doing whatever is expected from above, at the same time avoiding actions that upset the apple cart and lead to criticism. To be a good organization man or woman, in other words, is a reflection of the personal need to be popular and "in." Thus, this individual is unlikely to generate a burning involvement of the sort that evokes experimental or innovative approaches. Subordinates are expected to do little more than put forth average effort, to "belong," and to conform.

9,9   Figure 3.6 identifies the motivational dynamics of a 9,9 orientation. The plus pole involves contributing to important life goals and outcomes with and through others, which, in turn, aids them to be effective and happy as well. The minus pole relates to avoiding actions based on selfishness, such as occur when an individual views a situation to see how personal gain can be achieved without consideration for other people.

FIGURE 3.6

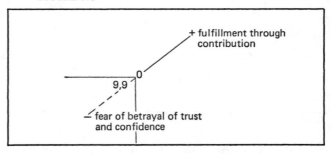

Fulfillment through contribution can be considered from two perspectives. One is what the individual is able to contribute to the situation in which he or she performs. The other is enabling others to contribute their resources toward problem solving and decision making in the fullest possible way. When a manager acts according to a sense of purpose and in a spontaneous, self-generating, and self-directing way, organization purpose and the individual's commitment to contributing are integrated. The consequences of 9,9 management are that subordinates also develop personal commitment to contributing to organization achievement. Involvement is generated in people who are able to combine their efforts to accomplish meaningful, productive goals.

These five motivational systems, then, constitute the "striving to reach" and "seeking to avoid" that characterize human behavior in modern society.

FIGURE 3.7

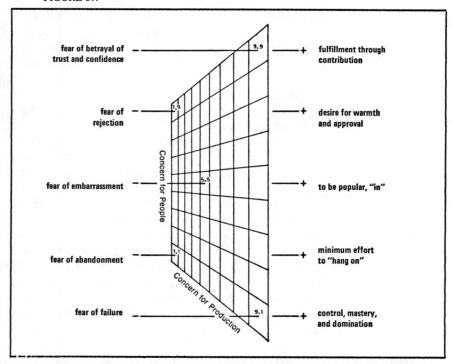

Source: *Grid Approaches to Managing Stress,* by Robert R. Blake and Jane S. Mouton. Springfield, Illinois: Charles C. Thomas, 1981.

Source: Robert R. Blake and Jane S. Mouton, *Grid Approaches to Managing Stress* (Springfield, Illinois: Charles C Thomas, 1981).

Now back to the big picture. When put together as the three-dimensional Grid, as illustrated in Figure 3.7, we can see the complexity and variety of human adjustments in a way that allows us to study and understand them as they apply to our own lives and to those whom we supervise.

Another Look at the 9,9 Orientation

One of the gains in understanding behavior made possible by the motivational axis is that of sorting out individual differences among people. For example, those oriented in a 9,1 way do not all manage in the same manner. A person who lives at the extreme of 9,1+, and for whom 9,1⁻ is an underdeveloped motivation, is likely to be a risk-taker, ready to go for "broke," gambling all in pursuit of domination, mastery, and control. To gamble and to lose may be a demonstration of failure to others, but for the person who lives at 9,1+, failure only spurs a more intense effort. The premise is that if you don't succeed, try, try again.

The opposite is characteristic for a person who is anchored at the extreme of 9,1⁻. For this person, failure is equivalent to self-destruction. Risk, in the sense of gambling or taking a chance on an outcome, is far too threatening. The person at 9,1⁻ prefers to avoid failure and in this way to "prove" strength.

Thus, we see two people who appear different, yet both manage according to 9,1 assumptions. At 9,1+ we see managers who are daring and unconventional; at 9,1⁻ we see managers who are disciplined and conservative. Both give close supervision because both distrust others. The 9,1+-oriented person is prepared to gamble, but he or she alone calls the shots and expects compliance. The 9,1⁻-oriented person is unprepared to gamble, but wants to ensure that no subordinate rolls the dice, either.

1,9

The motivational axis of 1,9+ brings out distinguishing features among managers, all of whom have the same basic 1,9 orientation. The individual whose orientation is 1,9+ actively pursues love, affection, and approval. Rather than feeling rejected when the wanted response is not forth-coming, this person feels compelled to be even more charm-ing and to do whatever is essential to increase the likelihood of gaining love from others.

The manager whose orientation is 1,9⁻ meets the first evidence of rejection as verification of unworthiness. This leads to greater and greater efforts to reduce further rejection by avoiding repetition of whatever is thought to have caused the initial rejection. A person in a 1,9⁻ orientation is likely to be immobilized or in retreat, to "stop" whatever has produced rejection.

1,1

A person adopting a 1,1⁺ orientation increases the likelihood of "hanging on" by taking on the outer behavior trappings that are expected, applauding on cue but without personal feelings for or convictions as to the validity of the action to which the applause is given. Because the socially approved reactions are given on signal, a person at 1,1⁺ avoids drawing attention to self and in this way increases the likelihood of hanging on, even though emotions of po-sitive identification may long since have been withdrawn.

A person who tends toward the 1,1⁻ end is likely to let things slide, unaware of the extent to which a sense of hopelessness and helplessness has blinded him or her to the realities of life. Only under sharp and jolting recognition of how far out one has gone are efforts likely to be pursued to avoid ultimate expulsion.

5,5

The motivation of the 5,5⁺ orientation is popularity, being in good standing with one's colleagues; feeling se-cure, confident, and even elated at one's own popularity. When successful, this results in a sense of well-being. A 5,5⁺ orientation lets a person develop the social skills of a "hail-fellow-well-met" kind of person. A 5,5⁺-oriented person does whatever others suggest or request in support of membership in "the group"; he or she may even initiate activities that appeal to others but that they did not expect, thus leading to the "What a great guy!" reaction.

The motivation of 5,5⁻-oriented persons involves fear of loneliness. Loneliness is a feeling of being deprived of wanted friendships, a sense of uneasiness at not being emotionally attached to others, yet not knowing why. Fear of loneliness can turn into despair when a person is unable to derive security from being with others. Fear of loneliness leads to avoiding any action that might result in separation. The person operating from such a 5,5⁻ orientation avoids any thought or action that could result in ridicule or becoming the butt of other's jokes; anything, in other words, that might push that person toward the margin of membership. The person with a 5,5⁻ orientation avoids taking a separate stand; cracking a joke, the point of which might not be evident; or drawing subtle inferences that might be wrong. In other words, cautiousness characterizes the person with a 5,5⁻ orientation. Others may see this person as lacking in "imagination."

9,9

A person who manages in a 9,9⁺ orientation is characterized by a "can do" spirit of confidence, a readiness to design experiments to find best solutions, and, therefore, by creativity and capability for being innovative. A 9,9⁺ orientation, in other words, is likely to result in a person being seen as brilliant. Brilliance may result less from native intelligence than from skill in learning.

A manager who supervises in a 9,9⁻-oriented manner is characterized by avoiding feelings of selfishness. This person is likely to deny his or her objective contribution, to take no credit for deserved achievement, and to make every effort to give it to others. This reaction may be seen as excessively modest.

3-D Grid

What does the *fulfillment-through-contribution* motivation mean in the day-in, day-out activities of management and supervision? How is avoidance of selfishness, the 9,9⁻ motivation, to be understood?

The first word, *fulfillment,* contains the key. Fulfillment means a person has good feelings that come from making a difference through helping others. The person is doing whatever needs to be done to aid others to be stronger, more effective, more autonomous, and more productive. Making a contribution involves actions that strengthen results, production, or profit. This reflects an attitude of concern for making the organization stronger, more effective, and more capable of competing with other companies. A word for this basic attitude is *identification.* When a person has identified him or herself with the organization's success, this individual has already crossed into personal involvement. Then it is "natural" to exert effort to help the organization become better. A member feels "good" because of a sense of personal contribution.

This motivation is akin to altruism. However, altruism is "total" selflessness, whereas a 9,9+ motivation is a matter of priorities. The need for contribution is motivating in its own right; the reward for making it, though not unimportant, is secondary. A person who is committed in this manner feels the importance of doing the right thing well, regardless of whether a reward for doing it is anticipated; however, consideration of the possible reward is not absent, as it is in the case of "pure" altruism.

The 9,9+ motivation's avoidance of selfishness suggests another difference between a 9,9 motivational system and altruism. An altruistic person seeks no external source of gain. Indeed, this individual is unaware that there is such a prospect. There is thus no basis for selfishness. By comparison, personal gain, particularly in the sense of fulfillment, is part and parcel of managing in a 9,9+ way. Thus, we speak of "enlightened self-interest" or altruistic egotism. This motivation produces an attitude of mind that causes a person to say, "I want to do this because I know it is the right thing to do. It is valuable, sound, and valid in its own right. Therefore, it should be done, not because I will gain from it, but because it will make a contribution." The second thought, of self-benefit, though present, is neither dominant nor primary. That is what distinguishes it from the 9,9⁻ motivation, where benefits may be gained by others but the action is undertaken with the primary motivation being personal gain. This is what a 9,9⁺-oriented person seeks to avoid.

Not all employees talk about feelings of identification with a company. Many even deny having such feelings. Some separate their positive feelings for colleagues from their negative feelings about the company itself, toward which they may feel genuine antagonism. Yet we know that such feelings of identification with the company and with colleagues and associates are more widespread than acknowledged. This is evidenced in how much people enjoy talking about their companies and their jobs.

The fact that some identification is present is the cornerstone for helping organization members develop a stronger 9,9 sense of fulfillment through contribution. The chapters that follow detail some of the 9,9 approaches to management that make it possible to strengthen and build skills based upon this source of personal motivation.

4
Communication

Communication is based on the assumption that mutual understanding is the key to agreement. When people genuinely want to know what is going on, they first need to explain, in a forthright and candid manner, exactly how they perceive the situation. Free two-way exchanges stimulate openness, trust, and spontaneity, and reduce the likelihood of conflict.

A remark by a senior manager identifies 9,9 attitudes toward communication. His comment was, "In the final analysis, words have no meanings; it is only people that have meanings." In effect, he was saying that problems of communication actually are problems of *exchanges between people*. Words are tools for achieving effective interplay, for communicating attitudes, feelings, and meanings. There is no problem of communication, per se. There are problems of people who work together trying to communicate with one another.

The power that a boss has and the way it is wielded in a boss/subordinate relationship is the key to communication problems. A boss who says to a subordinate, "Can we get together? I am interested in your ideas," is likely to be reflecting a 9,9 orientation. If a subordinate has reservations and doubts, these can be brought out before they fester and become chronic sources of resistance. If the subordinate has suggestions, they can be given, listened to, and dealt with rather than stifled. This approach stimulates subordinates to initiate contact when they think they have something to contribute.

At the very heart of the communication process are four issues: asking questions, listening and hearing, responding to a subordinate's point of view, and handling emotions.

Asking Questions

People gather information they want from many sources, such as books, newspapers, TV, and other communication media. Subordinates, as an example of those with whom you work, possess unique pieces of information that you need and want. Your access to this information is provided by asking questions in such a way that the answers will help you understand not only the facts but also the desires, needs, and motivations of subordinates. Questions allow you to test levels of knowledge and to determine what subordinates' expectations are. Questions are the door through which you can pass into others' minds to become acquainted with what they are thinking and why they are thinking it.

Questions are used to keep a discussion on target. They should be an integral part of your communication. Posing questions can be tricky, however. If they are good questions, you can get the kind of information you want. However, if questions are not good, strong, and meaningful, then they tend to do a disservice.

Direct Questions

If questions are used in a sound way to control conversation, it follows that we should learn not to use "uncontrollable questions." These are usually trite, evoke no intelligent response, and are without real pertinence to the objective. Some examples of such questions are: "What do you think?"; "Why did you do that?" The first one leads nowhere in particular and is, therefore, unlikely to evoke specific information. The second question places those being questioned in a defensive position, resulting in their wanting to withdraw from the conversation.

The following questions are ones that require a specific response.

- Who can give us this information?
- What time is most convenient for us to meet?

However, they are controllable within the limits of the question only. They do not provide adequate alternatives. An example of changes to make these questions even more controllable would be to rephrase them as follows.

- I suggest we call ABC Company or XYZ Company. Either one can give us the information we need.
- Would it be more convenient for you to meet with me at 3:30 or 4:30 today?

When properly formulated, direct questions can yield valuable information.

Opinion-Seeking Questions

Some opinion-seeking questions do not lead to reasonable involvement of the person questioned. They are dead-ended in that they prompt Yes/No answers.

- Don't you think we should go with Brand Z?
- Do you like this assembly flow design?

The person questioned can easily answer yes or no, but the desired response has already been implied. As an alternative to stimulate discussion, perhaps one could word the questions in the following ways.

- Bill, tell me, will your people be able to use Brand X to reduce their administrative work?
- Would this layout have possibilities as far as the production needs of your unit are concerned?

Fact-Finding Questions

Answers to relevant fact-finding questions are most helpful to both the boss and the subordinate.

- Did you get an answer yet from Mr. Smith about the proposal?
- By what date will you have the plans completed?

Such questions are thought-provoking and controllable. They invite participation and involvement.

Questions should be stated so they stimulate subordinates to mentally focus on the particular part of the issue that you are concerned about and think about it in relation to their understanding of the problem. By creating a plan for questions in your mind, the answers to which will strengthen your knowledge and understanding, you will be prepared to ask such questions in a logical sequence as the discussion progresses. However, it is possible to be too inquisitive and make your subordinates feel they are being put through the third degree. Skilled questioning can stimulate subordinates to think in a deeper, more constructive way.

Context of Questions

Questions can be asked in such a way that the total context of the inquiry is known to the other person as the basis for helping him or her form the answer. The question, "When can you give me the report on your department?" is far different from, "The annual report is scheduled for typesetting on January 15. My deadline for summarizing the year is December 15. When can you give me the information for your department?" In the second instance the questioner has provided the other person with background that enables the respondent to understand the context of the query. The first question gives no background for appreciating the questioner's circumstances or the context in terms of which the answer is relevant. The person questioned has the possibility of setting priorities for completion of the report, and the second form of the question invites him or her to do so.

Questions Versus Interrogation

There is another angle in this question business. A

boss can make subordinates feel weak by asking questions they cannot answer. Whether a subordinate *should* be able to answer the questions is beside the point; it is what the subordinate *thinks* about his or her inability to answer them that counts. It is easy for a knowledgeable boss to overwhelm the subordinate with a display of wisdom that will make the subordinate feel humiliated and resentful at being "given a test." This technique is used by a boss who believes intimidation is the best way to motivate subordinates to work harder or to do more. Questions that are too easy run the risk of being viewed by subordinates as so trivial that they are a waste of everyone's time. On the other hand, questions that are meaningful and pertinent enable a subordinate to contribute to the solution of problems and to provide a basis for the boss to test the subordinate's understanding of any proposition. By being open and aboveboard with respect to intentions, a boss is creating in the subordinate readiness to establish a relationship based on openness and trust. If both boss and subordinate have confidence in each other and the subordinate is asked a difficult question that he or she is unable to answer, the subordinate can say so without feeling incompetent or humiliated and with the understanding that assistance will be provided to help answer the question.

Facts Versus Evaluation

Still another angle on questions is this: Although some questions are asked to acquire factual information, others are evaluative. The latter questions call upon your subordinates to exercise judgment, to compare and to combine facts, and to expose opinions. There are no quick yes/no answers to them. These are the questions that are indispensable in sound management. They aid the boss in understanding the character of subordinates' thinking. Such understanding is important in assisting the the boss to come to a sound decision. In addition, these thought-provoking questions promote subordinates' participation and involvement and provide more of a problem-solving approach to the exercise of personal responsibility.

Asking questions, then, is a central feature of good communication. Questions can bind and bond a relationship, rather than weaken it. They can cement a conviction, rather than produce uncertainty. They can tie people together, rather than tear them apart.

Listening and Hearing

Certainly management involves situations where the boss does the talking and the subordinates listen. Yet a good discussion is a two-way street, a give-and-take of thoughts and attitudes, of ideas and opinions, of feelings and emotions. It leads to a meeting of minds. Yet there are many discussions in which the boss gets detoured or goes down a dead-end street. This is done, not by virtue of any defect in the need to solve a problem, but because of poor listening.

Listening and hearing can be two very different things. From the boss's perspective, agreement with his or her ideas can be achieved through 9,9 listening on the part of the subordinate and by sound, logical, and persuasive talk. What needs deeper analysis is the boss's listening and hearing skills. First, listening does not simply mean being quiet while the subordinate talks. Second, listening can be biased. What is heard is not necessarily what is said, and this is due to two factors. One is the character of the message. The other is the character of the listening. When a person talks, words must be found that will express thoughts and feelings. These words are not necessarily full statements of what a person is thinking or feeling. These words represent thoughts and emotions, but they are not "it." In fact, they can be poor substitutes. Because thoughts are formed in words and expressed in words, the expression of these thoughts can be clear, obscure, or anything in between. Emotions are felt by the speaker as the thoughts are expressed. Words, in themselves, may carry very little indication of those emotions across to the person who hears them, unless the receiver is very attentive to every sign that the speaker displays.

As a result, whenever a person listens to what is being

said, he or she must read between the lines and piece together, if possible, the totality of the speaker's ideas and feelings. The listener is free to ask questions. Depending on how these inquiries are phrased and how they are answered, they may ensure that the interpretation of what is being said is the interpretation that the speaker intended to convey. At a deeper level, the listener's receptivity is a function of personal nature. No person listens in a completely objective way. It would be impossible to do this. What is heard may equally be determined by what is inside the listener. The message that comes in must mix with a mass of experience, emotions, and attitudes, gaining new color from what has gone on and is going on in the listener's own mind. To the degree that the listener is able to sort out and keep personal opinions separate from what is being said, he or she is listening attentively.

The importance of all this is that listening is at least as important as talking. To listen accurately, the boss must seek the melody, not just the tone. One must grasp the meaning, not just the words; analyze the intentions, not just the language. When this is done successfully, the boss is far more likely to engage in a successful problem-solving discussion, deal with reservations, and give sound answers to questions.

The prime ingredient of 9,9 listening is the knowledge that the essence of thought and feeling is never captured in words. Words are less-than-perfect tools of communication, and the boss needs genuinely to understand what the subordinate genuinely means within the context of the other person's nature and circumstances. For this reason, the 9,9-oriented manager would be more likely to repeat the question or statement of convictions made by the subordinate for verification, not in the subordinate's exact words but according to the boss's understanding of those words. In this way the boss can be assured of genuinely understanding, to the fullest extent possible, what the subordinate really meant. By doing this, the 9,9-oriented manager is in the best position to be able to respond to the conveyed message according to the needs of the speaker.

The boss summarizes frequently to ensure that both parties remain on the same wavelength.

The 9,9 approach to listening is characterized by the manager's high fidelity. This manager is unlikely to screen or distort what is being said by mingling personal views with the subordinate's in such a way as to misinterpret or attach false emphasis to what the subordinate is saying. The boss is able to keep personal feelings separate so that they do not affect the capacity to hear in a valid way.

Responding to a Subordinate's Point of View

A problem-solving discussion between boss and subordinate, no matter how smoothly it flows, never corresponds exactly to the path of development in a boss's mind. A sound understanding and the readiness to agree with conviction to a solution may still be lacking on the part of the subordinate.

There are many possible thoughts and emotions that can occur to a subordinate while participating in a discussion. The subordinate quite often feels like commenting and may do so. Remarks that break the flow of discussion may come at any time. Some of them are relevant to what is being said at the time, but the boss may fail to see the connection. Others are in the form of general objections to what the manager is proposing.

Interruptions in a conversation need to be studied and taken notice of because they are important indications that the subordinate's point of view is at variance with that of the manager.

A 9,9-oriented manager appreciates that life is more than logic. Problem solving should be guided by logic, but life is felt through emotions. While constructively seeking to find solutions to problems, the 9,9-oriented manager appreciates that subordinates have needs and emotions, feelings and frustrations. All of these may pull discussions away from the straight path of logic. This manager does not see such departures from the shortest path as unnecessary detours, but rather as a normal part of the complexities of working with people as individuals.

Whatever the reason for a subordinate's interruption, a 9,9-oriented manager has respect for the individual's feelings. The interruption may not seem to bring out any new and important information on the subject, but it certainly is important from the subordinate's standpoint. So a 9,9-oriented manager feels it is important to understand what the subordinate is saying and why an interruption occurred at that particular point. A manager who takes this kind of diagnostic attitude is in a sound position to appreciate the subordinate as a person by comprehending how the individual thinks, what he or she thinks about, and why. Much of this analytical information is of value in aiding managers to see how their own points of view can be presented to their subordinates so as to make them as clear and understandable as possible. These managers realize that no two persons have exactly the same patterns of thought and that every person is distinctive in his or her own experience and emotions, a unique person with unique needs.

In any event, a 9-9-oriented manager would not attempt to insist that the subordinate must always remain on the subject. To be irritated at apparently aimless meandering or by disconnected statements that seem to have no bearing on the topic of discussion is only to lose sight of the deeper possibilities of attaining a true meeting of minds. Understanding the reason for the interruption can be a key to holding a subordinate's attention and gaining involvement. It indicates to subordinates that their thoughts, ideas, opinions, and feelings are acknowledged as important to the manager.

Handling Emotions

If life were all logic, the biggest barriers to human effectiveness would not appear. But rationality is not the strongest force in human affairs. Logic finds solutions to problems and gets things done; but emotions supply the power. They are the engine, the wellspring, the cause of action.

Now, we turn our attention to emotions as they exist in you and to what you can do, constructively, in living with your emotions. When a sound understanding of your own emotions has been gained, you will be in a much better position to be helpful in dealing with others who are being driven by their emotions rather than guiding themselves steadily through reasoning and logic.

Where do emotions come from and why do people have them?

Emotions are present in animals as well as in human beings. They serve a purpose. Negative emotions arise as signals to a person that things are not right, that danger lies ahead, that risk to life and limb may be in the offing. In modern society, these life-and-limb risks are not as great as they once were, of course, but risks to one's sense of well-being are probably greater now than formerly. The circumstances of living have changed, but every person still has deep reservoirs of emotions. The complex social environment today provides more than enough stimulation to provoke some of the most negative of human emotions as responses to threats to well-being. On the positive side, there are emotions of love and enjoyment of one's job, of excitement in performing it well. These positive emotions arise when people feel secure, successful, and effective. They surface when individuals are able to master situations that confront them, thereby strengthening their confidence in their ability to deal with future situations.

If your emotions are out of tune with the situation, they undoubtedly will get in the way of your establishing a sound relationship with subordinates. This is why it is important to look deeply into the whole matter of emotions and feelings.

First of all, in a 9,9 approach emotions are genuine. They are valid responses to situations that are being viewed from an objective orientation. A 9,9-oriented person can experience emotions of antipathy toward those responsible for injustice or feel emotions of affection for those capable of responding with affection. This person can feel the plight of people who are uninvolved and withdrawn and can comprehend with understanding the conservative, emotional, "playing it safe" attitudes of individuals whose emotions are always in the middle. People who operate according to a 9,9 orientation can challenge situations that are wrong and acknowledge situations that are right because they have learned that their emotions are a trustworthy source of self-judgment. This knowledge provides a basis of self-confidence for coping constructively with situations across a whole spectrum of encounters.

People who can handle their emotions in a 9,9-oriented way are often able to enrich even further their capacities for strong, yet sound emotional response, once they have a fuller and deeper understanding of this orientation. One of the key ways is helping others to be more comfortable through responding in 9,9 ways themselves. For example, a manager might say to a subordinate who is up in arms in a 9,1 temper reaction, "Hey, let's cool it. Let's sit down and discuss this situation and examine what is causing the difficulty." This coolheaded, constructive approach helps bring the logic of reality back into focus for the person who has lost control of emotions. If someone's emotions are of a 1,9 variety, the 9,9-oriented manager can help this person experiment in staying with situations that have more conflict and hostility in them, giving support and encouragement while the person learns to cope with such situations. The manager can challenge a subordinate whose emotions are of the 1,1 kind to look at himself or herself more clearly and to question whether or not a wrong turn has been taken. A 5,5-oriented person can be encouraged to venture into deeper commitment, to cope with the strongest currents that may be flowing beneath the surface. In doing each of these things, a 9,9-oriented person is enriching his or her own emotional strength while, at the same time, gaining insights that increase personal strength and effectiveness.

The most important thing that a 9,9-oriented person can do is apply skill in facing up to situations that have conflict in them. This consists of bringing the emotions that are being expressed into line with the objective requirements of the situation in a sound manner by critiquing the things in one's own behavior that may be creating barriers and by inviting others to provide critiques to gain further insight.

These deep emotional undercurrents, although always present in life, are not well understood by most people, but they can become understandable. A person does not gain much help from another who simply says to act naturally or to "be yourself." However, persons can get help and strength from others through readiness to let themselves be challenged; to challenge others; to critique and, most importantly, to listen to the feedback that is widely available. It is essential that a person turn on nature's hearing aid to learn what others are prepared to say.

SUMMARY

It is important for us all to know that communication has a two-way character. Like other properties of social systems, communication tends toward an equilibrium between the amount given and the amount received. For example, if an individual seeks a great deal of information but gives only a small amount, the system is unstable. It is not likely to retain the character of one communicator asking much but giving little and of the other giving much but receiving little. It is likely to drift in the direction of neither getting nor giving much. In a two-way exchange of information, openness and trust on one side stimulates openness and trust on the other; closedness stimulates closedness; hostility provokes counterhostility. If an individual genuinely wants to know what is gong on, he or she needs to tell, in a forthright and candid manner, what it is that is understood about the situation. This is *leveling*. Mutual understanding as the basis for agreement about a situation and how to deal with it places a high premium on open, two-way communication.

Based on their personal histories and experiences, individuals are likely to listen through filters that are unique to themselves. People tend to hear what they want to hear and disregard what they consider irrelevant, trivial, or unimportant. What appears trivial to one person, though, may seem more significant to another. Furthermore, most people listen defensively to negative information, explaining away or justifying what they may need most to comprehend and understand to increase personal effectiveness. Rationalization, projection, compensation, and other widely known mechanisms of defense come into play in the everyday dealings of bosses and subordinates. Once conditions promoting full disclosure have been achieved, there are few reasons remaining for misunderstandings, for withholding negative information, or for any of the many other communication pitfalls that are likely to arise as barriers to full effort. The goal of two-way communication is to be able to talk candidly and trustfully, and to communicate negative as well as positive information.

5
Confrontation

Conflict can hinder individuals in their efforts to contribute to organization objectives. From that standpoint it is unproductive. Yet conflict can promote innovation, creativity, and the development of new ideas that make organizational growth possible. From these standpoints, conflict is useful. The issue, then, does not lie in whether conflict is present but, rather, in what its sources, causes, and purposes are.

The 9,9 approach to conflict rests on the assumption that although conflict is inevitable and, indeed, desirable, it is also capable of being understood and resolved. The key rests in the way conflict is managed.

The best way to approach conflict is to anticipate it and take steps to ensure understanding and agreement before people take positions and freeze to them. Yet when conflict does arise, the 9,9 approach is to confront the issues and emotions in the interest of finding the best solution.

Confrontation is a means of focusing on antagonisms that are created by strong win-lose kinds of disagreement, facing up to them, and bringing them out into the open where they can be resolved directly by those who are a party to them.

Emotions that usually accompany conflict—anger, hostility, fear, anxiety, doubt, and disappointment—can also be dealt with directly.

There are two distinct meanings in the way that the word confrontation is used, and because there is no good substitute for this term, it is important to distinguish between them.

Two Meanings of Confrontation

Confrontation as Combat

One meaning of confrontation is a little beyond contest but falling short of actual combat. It rests upon the concept of bringing opposing points of view into sharp focus. This definition of confrontation is motivated by a wish to test one's strength against that of another. The underlying assumption is that one view or person will prevail over the other.

Confrontation as Comparison

This quite different meaning of confrontation involves bringing opposing points of view into the same sharp focus, but now with the aim of resolving differences through understanding and agreement. There is no commitment to the idea that one or the other point of view must prevail. The result may be that one point of view will prevail. If this occurs, however, it is because the other party to the situation has learned that there are necessary and sufficient reasons for accepting one position and rejecting the other. It may be that neither point of view will prevail. Out of the comparison and contrast, an emergent position is identified that incorporates something of both prior positions but adds an element of uniqueness that makes the third position superior to either of the others. It is possible that an entirely different solution, one that was recognized in neither initial point of view, will eventually be identified and found to be the soundest one.

Viewed by an observer, confrontation-as-combat and confrontation-as-comparison might appear highly similar. There is, however, an important underlying difference, often recognized only by those engaged in a confrontation. In the case of confrontation-as-combat there is a contest of wills—the holder of one point of view feels threatened by the holder of the other. In this kind of confrontation yielding means being forced by one's own weakness to accept a resolution. Losing is to be avoided.

The meaning of confrontation-as-comparison, using it for the purpose of drawing contrasts, implies the presence of trust in the relationship of those who are trying to resolve the difference. Trust implies goodwill and good intentions. To prevail is unimportant; to find a sound solution is all-important. Under these conditions, one person's yielding to the position of another is not capitulation. It entails no loss of face. It is no measure of weakness. Rather, it is the opposite of these things, a demonstration of commitment to a best solution arrived at by the use of logic and reason and by an understanding of emotions.

Confrontation in its first meaning is related to the kind of win-lose power struggle that frequently occurs when one or both protagonists have a 9,1 orientation. Confrontation-as-comparison, the second meaning, is motivated by an orientation toward 9,9 fulfillment through contribution.

The distinction between these two meanings of confrontation can be drawn simply and clearly: the first is based on answering the question "Who is right?" the second, "What is right?"

The following example portrays a situation between the headquarters executive vice president and the vice president of research and development who heads up the R&D subsidiary. The cleavage is brought about by a widespread feeling in operations that R&D people, while qualified in the sense of technical expertise, resist applying their efforts to real-life problems that can make a short-term difference to the profitability of the company. This has resulted in major operating facilities developing their own informal, but problem-centered, R&D departments. The subsidiaries see this as an unnecessary expense that can be avoided if the R&D organization becomes more responsive to their real needs.

The executive vice president arranges a meeting between himself and the vice president of research and development. He introduces the topic in the following way.

Exec. VP: The problem of identifying legitimate issues for the research and development effort has become a chronic source of friction in this organization.

VP, R&D: We're aware of that, but we also know people in the field are not in a good position to judge the long-range contribution that comes from us.

Exec. VP: Wait a minute, Jim. That is the very attitude that leads us into disagreement and conflict. There is an important problem here, and to bury it in generalities only ensures that the difficulty will persist and become more intense. The people in the field have real feelings. They have real perceptions. In my view, it is your job to earn their respect. We've got to face up to the problem. You have a significant task before you. Either you convince them that your R&D effort is the best for our company or you subject your effort to an objective study by external experts who are in a position to make a more factual determination.

VP, R&D: We're in a period of transition. A new crop of R&D department heads will be appointed in the next two or three years. Personally, I would like to do what you propose, but it is a three-step process. First, you and I and the operations people who use our work convene so that we can get their views and reactions. Step 2 occurs simultaneously but independently: we arrange for expert consultants to study us and give us their external view.

Exec. VP: Would you expose the Alpha project and the Delta project to outside experts?

VP, R&D: No. Nor to the internal users of our research. This is a board-of-directors-level project. The security on it is too important to our own efforts to bring it to commercial status. As Step 3, you and I talk about responsibility for studying the research user's evaluation of our efforts and the expert consultant's report. If we agree, and the changes that are suggested are within our charter, I commit myself to bringing the changes about.

If we agree, and it calls for a change in our charter, we both present our recommendations to the board. If we can't agree, we are in trouble. I further agree to face that circumstance with you should it become a reality.

Exec. VP: What about the R&D projects going on in the field at this time?

VP, R&D: I think a big part of that problem is in distinguishing what R&D funds are best spent on and what projects are best done as technical engineering in the field. Our general attitude has been that if the problem is present in two or more locations, then, whether it's technical engineering or applied R&D, we should be responsible for it. If it's a problem in the field that requires experimentation to get an answer, even if only in one place, it's an important problem that we should be responsible for. I want to see this as an important agenda topic in the meeting between you and me and the research users. I don't think it's beyond our capacity to find solutions for any of these.

This is an example of confrontation-as-comparison. The vice president of research and development has committed himself and the executive vice president has agreed to confront their differences through direct comparison of points of view. The problem has been lifted from confrontation-as-combat to confrontation-as-comparison. The discussion has been shifted from a 9,1-oriented domination, mastery, and control of an operation to a 9,9 orientation involving contribution to the corporation.

Problem Solving and Confrontation

In the following example we can see how bad problem-solving methods can lead to the necessity of confrontation and how good problem-solving methods make it possible to avoid slipping into a win-lose orientation.

The vice president of manufacturing is meeting with the department heads. Engineering and maintenance, technical engineering, and purchasing are represented. The discussion focuses on the allocation of capital funds to the various plants. Plant requests have exceeded the amount budgeted for capital improvements.

VP, Mfg.: Representing your plant managers, each of you has proposed alternative and different projects that have an attractive rate of return on investment. But the capital expenditures required exceed the budgeted amount that is available. If we take the various percents of predicted return and realize that at best they represent approximations, it is probably unwise to make a decision on any project. In addition, each of you is ready to do or die for your projects, because you know that available monies are insufficient to fund everyone.

Dept. Head, Eng. & Maint.: I agree with you. Year after year we have accusations, recriminations, loud yelling, acrimony, and bad feelings when we try to make decisions on this topic.

Dept. Head, Purch.: That's true, but somehow decisions get made and they've been pretty good in the past.

Dept. Head, Tech. Eng.: I've not been impressed with them. People in my shop feel that politics prevail over profit.

VP, Mfg.: I could let you battle it out, or, as an alternative, I could make the decisions myself unilaterally. However, I believe we should set some meaningful criteria of judgment, and once we agree on them, apply them and let the chips fall where they may. We can only do this if we have everyone committed to the rules of the game and seek to apply those rules in an equitable manner.

VP, Eng. & Maint.: I can buy that. Not only is it a right way to proceed, but I can take it back to my plant and sell it.

General agreement is expressed. Thereafter competing interests are dealt with in this way. Sound and equitable decisions are reached, demonstrating the feasibility of making decisions where subordinate interests are set aside in the interest of superordinate goals. This points to (1) the value of criteria in neutralizing emotions and (2) the readiness of individuals to agree, regardless of their selfish interests, when the larger contribution is self-evident. This is an example of how good problem-solving skills make it unnecessary to battle a problem from a selfish vested-interest point of view.

Confrontation Between Boss and Subordinate

When a boss is directly involved in a conflict with a subordinate, the following concrete actions are suggested as ground rules for confronting the issues. The boss:

1   Describes to the subordinate his or her own thinking in such a way that subordinate does not feel personally attacked or put down.

2   Takes nothing for granted while the subordinate describes his or her ideas and feelings. In answering questions, the boss is full and forthright, with the result that suspicions related to the boss's position are reduced or have no opportunity to develop. In asking questions the boss may not get an answer immediately. If not, he or she returns to the issue at another time and continues to do so until a true understanding of the expressed and unexpressed attitudes of the subordinate has been obtained.

3   Challenges the subordinate's thinking regarding different courses of action, but only after the boss and the subordinate have reached a shared understanding as to the subordinate's basic values, needs, and assumptions.

4   Probes for reasons, motives, and causes that give the subordinate a clear and possibly different perspective on the issue.

5   Presents facts, data, logic, and counterarguments to help the subordinate test his or her objectivity.

6   Asks for facts, data, logic, and counterarguments in order to test his or her own objectivity.

7   Helps the subordinate see when a possible action would not be in his or her best interest.

8   Stays with the discussion in a persistent way and only concludes it when every avenue of resolution has been explored.[2]

The following example is a confrontation between a plant manager and a department head. This is a confrontation-as-comparison where the focal issue is an emotional one.

Dept. Head: Look, I've been accused of taking a selfish point of view on this thing and hiding good people rather than risking losing them through recommending them for promotion. I don't think this is true. I feel resentful at the accusation. In a nutshell, I feel hurt because, as I see it, I've gone all out to make my department as good as the best.

Plant Manager: I'm aware that you feel resentful and hurt because you think your efforts and motivations have been misunderstood. But the problem remains. As I see it, it has become a cause of increased friction. Bill, you can't badmouth other people and then turn around and complain that you are misunderstood.

Dept. Head: I don't badmouth other people. I'm careful that whatever I say is an accurate description of the way it is.

Plant Manager: Could it be the way you say it?

Dept. Head: I don't think so.

Plant Manager: We're in basic disagreement. I can't convince you of what I see the problem to be; you deny there is a problem.

Dept. Head: Well, there are always problems.

Plant Manager: No, you know what I mean Bill . . . . I've got a suggestion. Last month you brought in a new section head from outside. He has no reason to have a bias. Why don't you talk to him, independent of this discussion, and tell him the things we've talked about. If he has heard the same thing, then it would seem to me that you have to acknowledge that they're not just my opinions but are sufficiently widespread that a newcomer, who has no reason to choose sides, already has picked them up.

Dept. Head: That sounds like a fair test. If he is aware of them, I certainly do have a problem. If he's not, I may or may not, but I am willing to search out this information.

One week later

Plant Manager: What did you find out?

Dept. Head: You were right. The new section head has only been with us a month, and he's established respect as a hard worker and smart section head. He's an up-and-comer, and he's already worried because he's heard I deadened people by retaining them when I should have recommended them to you and others for broadening experiences or promotion. I do have a problem. I know it, and I know what to do about it. Thanks a lot.

This is a 9,9-oriented confrontation-as-comparison. The neutral source of independent data is a tip-off to the department head that results in his facing his own emotions and insecurities, which are basically of a 9,1 orientation. He wants to run the best department through domination and yet is motivated by fear of failure when he tries to release good people.

Confrontation at the Team Level

Conflicts often can be resolved on a one-to-one basis because they occur between and are limited to two people. This is not always the case, however,

Sometimes the conflict is teamwide. This occurs when everyone is stirred up and each has a solution that no one else is prepared to accept. The situation becomes even more intense when Member A comes to feel that it would constitute personal defeat if Person B's solution were to be accepted. When such tension exists between A, B, C, D, and E, the best that can be hoped for is compromise, and the worst is impasse, However, if conflict can be openly confronted by the team, resolution becomes possible, with advantages accruing from finding better solutions as well as retaining and strengthening the involvement of individual members.

Usually this only occurs when the boss brings it about. The boss may begin by posing the dilemma: "Each of us has a different view, and we each have our own hip-pocket solution. There is a more objective view somewhere, and a valid solution that can resolve the problem if we can find it. Our job is to step back and to try to understand why we are locked in. Bill, how do you see the problem, and how does this differ from what you've heard me and others say?"

Starting with Bill and moving around until all have aired their views and have proved they understand the positions and views of others is the first step toward cutting through subjective feelings and creating a greater readiness on the part of each member to consider objectively others' points of view.

Sometimes the blockage is caused by antagonisms that exist between one or more members. The "problem" becomes controversial, not because members are at a loss to deal with it but because they need the controversy to feed their emotional antagonisms. When this is so, the resolution is to get those who say "black" and the others who say "white" to recognize the antagonistic factor in their relationship; to examine openly what they are doing to foster it; to bring it to an end. Even when not directly involved in the controversy, the boss joins with subordinates to help the antagonists to work through their differences, challenging those in disagreement to explain to one another the reasons for it. Their reactions indicate whether or not they have understood the situation in the same way. If they have not, the boss keeps asking questions that allow them to confront their differences, presenting facts, counterarguments, and logic to help them test their objectivity. Once they come to understand their own values and assumptions, the boss can challenge their thinking and logic regarding the different courses of action available, probing for reasons, motives, and causes to give them a clear and possibly different perspective.

Sometimes team conflict erupts, not because of subjective attitudes or antagonisms, but because of a lack of team goals to which members are committed. Under these conditions each member pursues his or her personal goals and these may come into conflict. Now the solution is to get members committed to teamwide goals and to tailor their individual goals to the team goals in such a way that mutual support becomes, first, possible and then, a reality.

Though managers may realize that open confrontation is the most direct and valid approach to team and one-to-one conflict, they often shrink from bringing such a discussion about. This reluctance originates from several sources. The most important is the fear that the discussion may get out of hand and leave wounds that will not heal—that conflict, openly acknowledged, might escalate out of control. Another is the worry that the boss who initiates such a discussion will look weak, or actually lose control and be unable to resolve differences in a quieter, more sophisticated, "private" way. Another source of reluctance stems from a different value orientation that says the manager should mastermind the solution he or she wants and bring it into use on a "fait accompli" basis.

All of these are "real," but they are not valid reasons for avoiding confrontation as a means of conflict resolution. Through the exercise of good leadership, the discussion stays channeled and does not get out of hand. Once tensions are identified, the pressures and strains on those who feel them can be relieved. The boss who opens up such a discussion appears strong, not weak, because the boss shows confidence and skill in utilizing the resources of others in a problem-solving direction. Finally, by open discussion, rather than masterminding a solution, teamwide commitment is maintained and attention can be focused on consultation, exchange of viewpoints, and consensual resolution of differences.

SUMMARY

Regardless of whether conflict is between a boss and a particular subordinate or occurs within a team setting, confronting and resolving it is the approach employed by the 9,9-oriented manager. Versatility means that a manager can learn to maintain a 9,9 orientation in a consistent day-by-day way. It is not necessary to lapse into a backup Grid style, to become a situational manager, or to "solve" problems in a Machiavellian way. Tactics of conflict resolution vary with the situation, but the strategy of confrontation is maintained in a consistent manner.

6
Responsibility

The ability to make a maximum contribution is based upon a deep-seated capacity to resolve the dilemma of how to exercise responsibility for one's own actions in a voluntary, spontaneous way and still be able to act interdependently. The exercise of responsibility within any level in an organization is possible when the power and authority necessary for taking initiative is delegated. Thus, delegation by a person in a managerial position is necessary if those at subordinate levels are to be able to exercise self-responsibility. Delegation starts at the top, with each succeeding level releasing responsibility to those below. There are a number of good reasons why bosses should delegate responsibility. Yet frequently subordinates are heard to complain, "I can't take an action without checking with my boss." "The boss calls the shots." "It's not my responsibility because I don't have the authority to back it up."

Why Don't Bosses Delegate More?

There are several reasons why bosses make less use of delegation than is desirable and, therefore, fail to elicit the contributions subordinates could make under conditions of self-responsibility.

Lack of confidence that the subordinate will act responsibly under his or her own initiative

Many managers simply do not trust subordinates to handle delegated responsibilities. This lack of trust can be traced to many factors. However, it is true that when expanded responsibility is first accepted, the subordinate is at his or her weakest point. Previous experience may not have offered the practice necessary for carrying out the new assignment. Yet it is inevitable that if a person is to learn newly delegated responsibilities and to exercise initiative in carrying them out, the freedom to try, to experiment, and sometimes even to make mistakes is needed. The boss who feels distrustful of subordinates feels compelled to pull back on the first "blunder" by the subordinate and so withdraws delegation by the very act of solving the problem directly.

This attitude is widespread. It accounts for much of the underutilization of subordinates. By keeping the action centered on himself or herself, the boss is assured that the mistakes that otherwise might be made will be avoided. It is for this reason that the question frequently is asked, "Why is it that managers are typically running out of time while their subordinates are typically running out of work?"

Distrust is not easily erased. Several actions on the boss's part can help this situation. One is awareness of what happens at that point where a subordinate is in transition from less responsibility to more. Another is readiness to offer support through critique or discussion but to leave the ball in the subordinate's court. These can do much to aid the subordinate to see pitfalls and thereby avoid falling into them. They also provide a way for both boss and subordinate to be constructively involved in ensuring positive results from increased delegation.

Feeling of less importance when subordinates do more

Strange as it may seem, bosses report feeling less important when they see people who are subordinate to themselves doing what they previously did. This is particularly true when the subordinate does as well or better than the boss did. The boss's self-interpretation of this situation is: "I am not as indispensable to the organization as I once thought." This line of reasoning leads to a diminished sense of self-importance. When one holds all the strings, even though this leads to feeling harassed and under pressure, at least one preserves an image of self-importance. This is so even though preservation of that image may negatively affect the boss, the expansion of the organization, and the best interests of subordinates.

By "hogging" decisions that are dramatic and that will draw attention to themselves, bosses gain a feeling of remaining in the center of things. This adds to a sense of self-importance. Then bosses become even more unprepared to relinquish responsibility, preferring to keep important decisions for themselves, even though these decisions might be made as well or even better at lower levels.

Delegation reduces the need for firefighting and causes a person to appear unbusy

Firefighting means just what it says—putting out fires, dealing with one crisis after another. These are the unanticipated fires that pop up, creating a need for urgent solution. Many managers indeed have a need to experience this sense of urgency, because only then can they regard themselves as fully occupied and "giving the organization their all."

However, this compulsive need to be busy can be viewed as the need to avoid contemplation, quietness, being thoughtful, pondering possibilities, formulating alternatives, and doing many intellectual things that, in themselves, provoke no sense of urgency. "A man of action," which describes how so many managers see themselves, is therefore frustrated and threatened by the qualities of composure and contemplation that strategic thinking and planning require. By staying busy and taking a short-term, narrow-focused, firefighting posture, one is never confronted with the need to think abstractly, coherently, systematically, or strategically, even though this is what may be needed, from an organization point of view.

Anxiety about what is happening, with no "good" way of finding out

One of the discomforts bosses sometimes experience about delegation is a lack of knowledge about how things are going or what is happening. To find out what is going on may be viewed as "checking up" or looking over the subordinate's shoulder. These kinds of actions reveal that the responsibility is not truly the subordinate's. The boss continues to feel the pressures, and this contradicts the original purpose of delegating responsibility.

When subordinates are assigned increased responsibilities, they must inevitably have time to execute the actions that these responsibilities require and to do so without constantly checking back with the boss to relay how things are going or to ask for advice. As a result, a "hollow" period is created in which the boss may be getting no feedback whatsoever as to whether the situation is progressing nicely or whether, in fact, a subordinate's plans are faltering or even going to end in disaster. Without this knowledge, the boss becomes anxious and begins to probe to find out how the situation is moving. This probing in itself has the effect of undermining the subordinate's security. The subordinate may feel that such probing is unnecessary and, in fact, reflects a lack of confidence in his or her ability to get things done. In turn, this can have the effect of producing anxiety in the subordinate. When these situations of double anxiety come about, the boss probes to find out how things are going and finds uncertainty in the subordinate, which almost certainly will cause the boss to take back the responsibility from the subordinate.

Who has the responsibility?

Another aspect of delegation, which appears on the surface to support it, nonetheless prevents it.

Consider the situation where a boss who feels responsible and wants to be strong is approached by a subordinate who is confronted by a dilemma or has a problem. The subordinate may or may not ask for help directly. In any event the boss, in an act of support of the subordinate, unwittingly allows the problem to jump one level up. Before the boss knows it, the problem that the subordinate was trying to solve is now "owned" by the boss. For all practical purposes this is reversed delegation. It comes about by the subordinate provoking the involvement of the boss in solving problems that should remain the responsibility of the subordinate.

Once subordinates realize that whenever they are in trouble they can go to the boss and let the problem slide up one level, they are then assured of the lowered risk of passing it on for solution rather than failing in an attempt to solve it themselves. This has the effect again of creating a feeling of importance in the boss due to his being called upon to deal with the difficult problems. The subordinate is made weaker by virtue of his or her self-reliance being reduced when the going gets tough.

Delegation Skills

There is another set of reasons why organizations fail to take advantage of the benefits that can be derived from exercising delegation.

Many organizations seek to develop personnel through organized management development programs of a formal academic sort but also use the organization in a variety of ways for bringing about appraisals: the use of rotation across divisions, functions, geographic areas, or countries to give those capable of benefiting from it the widest possible exposure to situations and problems; systematic programs for aiding each person to develop primary and backup skills in more than one area; and a host of other mechanisms. However, these strategies are likely to make a positive contribution only to the degree that the boss immediately in charge of subordinates possesses the kinds of delegation skills that will aid subordinates to digest their experiences, learn from them, and in this way develop the strength necessary for autonomous action. What are some of these skills?

Delegation as continuous expansion of responsibilities

A boss, seeing the potential benefits of delegation, might arrange for a subordinate to be given broad new assignments that confront the subordinate with dealing with areas in which no experience has been gained. If this responsibility in an unfamiliar area is given to the subordinate all at once, the manager's assumption is likely to be that people either sink or swim and that those who swim are the good ones. This sink-or-swim concept of delegation has a 9,1-oriented flavor to it. It calls for subordinates to "prove" themselves to the boss, rather than the boss seeing it as his or her responsibility to the subordinate to develop talent rather than discover it.

The alternative is to increase delegation a step at a time, with each step of increased responsibility being sufficiently small as to be well within the subordinate's capacities for dealing with it, yet large enough to constitute a real challenge. Many times by thinking the situation through, a boss can see how increased responsibility can be passed to subordinates in a sequential way. The subordinate is provided with an opportunity to digest one new responsibility before being handed another. In this way a series of assignments that significantly expand the subordinate's responsibilities is delegated without any one assignment being so large as to be impossible. Thus, skill in expanding delegation on a sequential activity basis is an important consideration.

Delegation of simple activities before complex ones

By the same considerations, it is important that initial increments of responsibility consist of activities that are fairly simple to avoid taxing the subordinate's existing capacity for dealing with them. As the subordinate's capacity for managing greater responsibilities increases, it becomes possible to delegate activities that are of a more complex character. The boss has confidence that these new, complex activities can be handled because prior ones of somewhat lesser difficulty already have been successfully accomplished.

Using action research approaches for critique to learn from experience

One of the most useful skills to rely upon in efforts to increase delegation involves ongoing critique and re-planning of the enlarged assignment. What this means, in practice, is that the boss does not assign increased responsibility to a subordinate and then wait six months or a year to discuss the progress being made or the failures that have occurred. Rather, the skill required in aiding a subordinate to more effectively implement the activities associated with increased responsibilities is that of ongoing critique. This means that the boss, at appropriate occasions, explores progress being made with the subordinate and problems that are being encountered. These discussions do not consist of *telling* the subordinate how to solve problems or what to do. The purpose is to aid the subordinate to see situations confronting him or her from the viewpoint of a person who is more familiar with the problems and pitfalls that these situations inevitably contain. With this kind of action-research use of critique, objectives are set in the beginning when delegation occurs. Then as actions are taken, these actions are evaluated against the original objectives to see if they are sound. If not, the actions being taken are altered in some way to meet the original objectives. Then the original objectives are reviewed. If they are no longer sound, they are revised to be more consistent with the current situation, and future actions are planned on this basis. In this way the boss is able to continuously monitor and coach the subordinate in those activities with which the subordinate may not be as familiar as necessary. This kind of learning from experience through the use of ongoing critique builds strength into the learning cycle that can thereafter be relied upon as new responsibilities are assigned. Both boss and subordinate stand to benefit through this positive interaction.

There are a number of suggestions that can be offered to increase the effectiveness of delegation to subordinates.

Dos and *Don'ts* of Delegation

Don't delegate without development

As previously mentioned, one way bosses regard delegation is handing someone a new activity on the sink-or-swim premise. If the individual can do it, it will get done. If not, now is the time to learn. This is an old-fashioned notion, inconsistent with a sound concept of effective supervision.

Development comes first. To ask subordinates to accomplish tasks with which they are totally unfamiliar is to invite catastrophe. Rather, a boss should provide a subordinate with a series of experiences that allows for a grasp of the basic activity itself and how to carry it out. Through the sound use of teamwork, it is possible many times to involve a subordinate in participating in situations from which much can be learned, even though contribution may be small. This is one of the most excellent ways of all for aiding individuals to gain the insights essential for accepting delegation, once it comes their way. Confidence in a subordinate's abilitiy to take an assignment should come after development has provided the skill for doing it.

Don't delegate and continue to supervise

Another error that leads to ineffective delegation is asking subordinates to do something on their own initiative and responsibility and then continue supervising how it is done. This is delegation in form but without substance. In every practical way, the boss retains responsibility for the solution of problems. The implication that the activity has been delegated is a sham.

Don't delegate and retrieve

Also to be avoided is for the boss first to delegate and then, after finding that things have gone radically wrong, to retrieve the activity, taking it away from the subordinate and returning responsibility for completing the activity to himself or herself. Sometimes it is necessary to retrieve, but the unilateral tactic being described here is what should be avoided.

Don't set up a spy network

One of the common observations of bosses, particularly in the period immediately after an activity has been delegated to a subordinate, is that they lose touch with what is going on and do not wish to double check with the subordinate. Double checking is thought to convey a lack of trust and confidence. When a boss coninues to be anxious about what the subordinate is in fact doing, the temptation is to set up a spy network to find out what is really going on without directly confronting the person responsible for the activity. Spy networks never really work well. As people become aware that a spy network is in operation, they withhold information from it or feed information into it not necessarily based upon aiding the boss to know what is going on but equally as often based on preventing the boss from finding out what he or she wants to know.

Do set up an expectation of feedback with the subordinate

By setting up the expectation that feedback is desirable, the boss can ensure that performance is up to standards. This can be done in such a way as to avoid projecting the idea of distrust or lack of confidence. This kind of feedback is designed to keep the boss in touch with what is happening so subordinates will take advantage of experience and counsel when needed.

Do critique

Feedback is essential for critique, but it is only part of the total critique process. Critique means digesting data to learn and to derive generalizations that have wider application. By critiquing the difficulties subordinates encounter in newly delegated assignments, the boss finds it possible to help them learn without telling them what to do. Too, the boss strengthens the ability to work with other subordinates given increased responsibility.

Do retrieve when necessary

It is sometimes evident that a subordinate is in over his or her head, no matter how promising prior performance has been. It becomes apparent that the subordinate is unable to perform a previously assigned delegated activity in a satisfactory manner. To permit the subordinate to continue to make mistakes is unsound. Retrieving the delegated responsibility may be the most appropriate way to handle an over-delegated activity. The difference between the previous don't and this particular do is in the manner in which the retrieval is undertaken.

The sound versatility strategy for retrieving responsibility is that feedback, critique, and review lead to a joint decision that the delegated activity is being carried out in an unsatisfactory manner. Consensus is reached that the best solution is for the subordinate to be relieved of responsibility for the activity. This kind of jointly agreed-upon resolution of the problem ensures continued mutual understanding. It avoids the tensions that subordinates may otherwise feel when they are given opportunities only to have them taken away later.

In addition to providing the basis for self-responsibility, delegation is an important key to leadership, building a succession program, and expansion of any organization.

Key to Leadership

If a person in a leadership position is able to delegate, the act of doing so provides the time necessary to do those things that only a leader can do. Some of these include:

- thinking about the future and developing a preferred scenario for getting there;
- setting objectives with subordinates for current and future implementation;
- critiquing present and past performance and analyzing change possibilities;
- providing for subordinates' development needs;
- designing strategies for getting subordinates involved in their own growth and development;

■ ending the firefighting and crisis-management aspects of managing.

When the boss holds all the strings, exercises close supervision, approves every action, and is constantly giving or withholding an okay, time and freedom to think are simply not available.

Building a Succession Program

Delegation puts responsibilities on subordinates. When done well, these new activities are challenging but manageable. This stretch factor is important because it results in developing more and more people who can do more and more things. An additional contribution is that with the ever-increasing scope and responsibilities of subordinates, a reservoir of talent becomes available as opportunities for succession arise.

Expansion

New appointments and promotions are likely to arise more and more often when managers delegate well, not only because of normal attrition but also because managers who delegate have the time to plan, to see opportunities, and to act upon them. Then, when opportunities for expansion arise, a pool of talented and developing subordinates is available to be promoted into newly created responsibilities.

SUMMARY

In extreme cases the boss who fails to delegate responsibility to others holds all the strings, does whatever thinking is done, monitors execution in close detail, and produces weak subordinates who fail to exercise self-responsibility. The alternative is to exercise leadership through the development of subordinates. One of the most important ways of doing this is by the method of delegation.

Delegation frees bosses from everyday details and enables them to think, contemplate, plan, set objectives, and see possibilities they would otherwise be unaware of were they to be tied up in firefighting, close supervision, and in pursuing short-term objectives that could be handled by subordinates. Not only is delegation valuable for providing leaders with the freedom to do what leaders must do, it also strengthens day-by-day operations and the basis for succession. In addition, it creates the foundation essential for a business to expand.

There are a number of reasons why managers under-delegate and are overworked. These include distrust of subordinates, the fear that they will seem less important if those lower in the organization can do what they have been doing and do it as well or better, and, finally, the need that many bosses have to be ''helpful'' by taking over a subordinate's problems and solving them. In the latter case particularly, the boss may earn the subordinate's gratification, but only at the cost of reducing the subordinate's strength.

Another broad set of reasons for insufficient delegation is related to the fact that many bosses lack the skills that are essential for successful delegation. One of these involves sequencing delegation one step at a time. Another involves the need for grading delegation according to the ability of the subordinate, ranging from matters that are relatively simple, viewed from the perspective of the subordinate's initial capability, to matters that are realtively complex. A third involves ongoing critique, which aids the subordinate to learn from experience while carrying increased responsibilities. The result of such ongoing critique is that less and less help is required from others. Then, subordinates can rely on the initiative and confidence they gain from effective problem solving.

7
Shared Participation[1]

U tilizing dynamics of involvement through teamwork brings 9,9 contribution into play. With sound teamwork members can dig into, get at, and remedy underlying causes of operation problems. Teamwork is the key to seeing and seizing opportunities that otherwise might not be recognized. From the member's point of view, effective teamwork that emphasizes fulfillment through contribution is one of the basic sources of satisfaction that the industrial world has to offer.

Are You a Team Member?

The first issue that a manager might ask is, "Am I a member of a team?" Then, "If so, which one?" "Who are the other members?" Even though a manager shares a single boss with several colleagues, he or she might be tempted to say, "No, I am not a member of a team. The people who report to the same boss I do never meet together. We're a bunch of individuals. We're not a team."

Family Teams

Take another look. Here are some tests for whether you and others who report to the same boss are or are not a team.

Let's say you bring up a problem with your boss. You

are not a member of a larger team if the solution that is reached can always be implemented by you alone and if others who report to your boss have no need to know about it. If your job is that way, there are only two people on your team—you and your boss. If others who report to this boss deal with matters that only the boss and each of them can solve on a one-to-one basis, then there are several two-person teams but no larger one. This situation rarely arises except in certain staff situations where one boss oversees a number of disparate functions.

However, you are a member of a larger team if you bring a problem to your boss and you receive any of the following responses:

"Let me check this out with Bill first."

"Okay, but coordinate your action with Cathy."

"Don't worry. Don is taking care of that."

"Okay, but see Al so he'll know what's going on."

"Go ahead. Your action supports but does not overlap what they are doing."

If reaching a decision involves remarks such as these, then you are a member of a larger team. It includes you, your boss, and several colleagues. What you do touches at some point on what they do. You and they are interdependent.

You are also a member of a team if your boss says, "Do it, but don't tell anybody until it's finished. If they know in advance, they'll block it." This is an example of unsound teamwork. Members are working against the team and against one another, rather than supporting each other in their efforts to get results. Nonetheless, you are a member of a team, and there is a need for shifting the situation from a canceling-one-another-out point of view toward cooperative teamwork if the true potential is to be realized.

There is another test of whether you are a team member. Instead of making any responses like those above, your boss says, "Do whatever you want." Does this mean you are not a member of a team? No, not necessarily. You, your boss, and others may be members of the same team, but the teamwork is so lacking in quality that neither you nor your boss have a sense of belonging to a team. You should be operating as a team but you are not. The challenge is to become a team and to gain the benefits teamwork makes possible.

Matrix Teamwork

Of increasing interest in recent years is the matrix concept of organization. Under these arrangements at least two differently structured arrangements are possible. In one a subordinate may have more than one boss, such as a line reporting relationship and a functional specialty reporting arrangement. In another any member may belong to more than one team, often on a temporary basis but sometimes more or less permanently, such as a project team, a marketing launch team, or some other kind of interdepartmental grouping.

Matrix-centered structures place even greater emphasis on teamwork, as a member may join in to contribute his or her specialized expertise, then leave. If unable to work with others in a more or less spontaneous way, this member's contribution is likely to be reduced or completely canceled. Additionally, the member who cannot resolve tensions that arise from having two bosses also may be compelled to work at a level of reduced effectiveness. In the situation where one has a temporary boss, reliance on traditional concepts of power and cooperation and coordination no longer may hold.

Matrix teamwork involving 9,9 skills of participation enables members to contribute to organization effectiveness in a significant way. Fifteen criteria for answering the question, "Who should participate?" will be examined further on in this chapter. These criteria all apply with equal pertinence to composing a matrix-centered team.

There is one other way you may be a member of a team without recognizing it. For example, suppose you take a certain action and, because you have done so, other people automatically are able to act; or, because you took a certain action, others who might have acted in a certain way now have no need to do so. Things go smoothly and you do not notice how one person's effort helps another. This is very fine teamwork, even though you may not recognize it as such. It is different only because it happens sequentially.

Teamwork does not mean everyone meeting together all the time. It may occur when a person is operating alone, or with one, several, or all members. It may occur in a face-to-face situation, when each member is separated from every other, or when one person is out of the situation and another is acting in his or her behalf.

How Involvement Relates to Teamwork

1/All

Consider a team with four members. Al is the boss; Bill, Cathy, and Don are subordinates. Some problems can only be solved by Al, Bill, Cathy, and Don working on them together. Such situations are "one-to-all" (1/all). These 1/all problems bring together everyone who reports to the same boss to focus on and deal with a given problem to the solution of which every member can contribute. It involves teamwide participation. Thus, 1/all means everyone who is a member of a team is involved. This is simultaneous teamwork. It occurs when (1) no single member has enough knowledge, information, experience, breadth, or wisdom to formulate the "total" answer, but everyone working together can be expected to reach it; (2) coordination is required to get the job completed (every member has a piece of the action; therefore, each member's involvement is significant to a successful outcome); and (3) all must understand the overall effort so that individual ongoing activities can be structured accordingly. Planning a budget might be an example.

1/1/1

This is more complex but no less important. What happens is that each member takes a certain action that makes it possible for another member to take a second action, and so on, until everyone has contributed, in sequence, to the end result. It is a one-to-one-to-one (1/1/1) effort. Each team member's activity is indispensable, but in a predictable sequence. An example begins when a sales representative writes up an order. Smooth coordination from the salesperson through those who receive the order, those who fill it, those who prepare the invoice, and finally to those who help package and ship the order constitutes a complex sequence of interdependent operations. Done well, they satisfy the customer and build repeat business. Though there may be no face-to-face meetings, what the several people do links them together in a team effort. This is sequential teamwork.

1/Some

Here a successful outcome involves more than two people but not the entire team. These are 1/some situations. They fall between 1/1 (dealt with in the following paragraph) and 1/all and only differ in the number of members involved, rather than in the character of interdependence, whether simultaneous or sequential. Therefore, they will not be treated separately. This category is mentioned only to ensure that 1/some interactions are recognized as such and are utilized when needed.

1/1

Team problems that involve only Al and Bill together are 1/1 team actions. It is up to them to work out the solution and to take the actions that move the team toward its goals. These 1/1 actions between Al and Bill free Cathy and Don, who can contribute nothing, to use their time in dealing with other aspects of the overall situation.

In 1/1 situations any member may interact one at a time with any other member, according to that person's specific area of responsibility and need for help, support, data gathering, consultation, coordination, decision making, and so forth. Failure to bring in that other member can be expected to have adverse effects. Additionally, bringing in anyone other than that one other person would be wasteful, since additional members can contribute nothing. The mode of interdependence may be simultaneous, as just described, or it may be sequential.

1/0

Certain "team" problems involve *only* Al—or Bill, or Cathy, or Don—in the solution. The reasoning behind 1/0 is that Al has the responsibility, the capacity, and the information to solve the problem. Then it is in the interest of teamwork for Al (or whomever) to solve the problem alone and, thereafter, to let others know of his solution to the degree that it affects their own responsibilities. Such "team" problems, in other words, are "one-alone" (1/0) problems. Individual effectiveness contributes to teamwork by moving the team toward its goals and avoiding duplication of effort.

When there is understanding and agreement about the conditions under which a manager does not involve others, solo decisions are not seen as arbitrary or unilateral but as part of his or her responsibility. There is neither resistance nor resentment. These 1/0 actions may be carried out in private or in the presence of others. The point is that although they are not joint or emergent actions, they are still an essential part of good teamwork.

A special case of 1/0 occurs whenever one team member takes an action or substitutes himself or herself in behalf of another team member:

> I know you have to go to New York to arrange a loan. I'm going to see our R&D people up there next Thursday. I could also deal with the loan people and make it unnecessary for you to be away at the same time unless there is something more involved.

Another example is this:

> Bill is away on an extended foreign trip, but I can act in his behalf and give you an answer.

When this kind of 1/0 teamwork takes place, the initiative rests with whatever team member takes the supportive action, but the responsibility for outcomes remains with the member on whose behalf the action was taken. In this sense it calls for trust to a degree beyond that required in any other kind of situation.

Thus, 9,9 teamwork may occur under 1/all, 1/some, 1/1/1, 1/1 or 1/0 conditions, depending upon three fundamental aspects. One is related to decision quality. A second is concerned with the acceptance aspects involving readiness to implement the action called for. The third deals with management development. We are now in a position to examine when 9,9 team action should be 1/all, 1/1 or 1/0. This is an excellent example of maintaining a consistent *strategy* but shifting *tactics*, according to the requirements of the situation.

Testing Actions for When They Should Be 1/0, 1/1, or 1/All

Rules that clarify when to use 1/0, 1/1, or 1/all strategies are introduced in Table 7-1. These guidelines answer the question, "Under what conditions are 1/0, 1/1, 1/some, or 1/all approaches likely to be most effective?" The left-hand column identifies criteria that help a manager decide if 1/0, 1/1, or 1/all is the soundest basis of action. The conditions for 1/some are so similar to 1/all that they are not separated for discussion, but these are actions that involve more than 1/1 but less than 1/all, where "all" means the entire membership of the team.

A boss should act without consulting others when the criteria for good decision making and problem solving, shown on the left, match the conditions in the 1/0 column. When conditions match entries in the second column, 1/1 actions should occur. When the circumstances match those in the column to the right, 1/some or 1/all actions should be taken.

These first six criteria relate most closely in one way or another to maximizing the quality of decision making by the effective and efficient use of human resources.

1 Responsibility for the Problem. If, in viewing a problem, an individual can say, "That problem is my sole responsibility, and I have the capacity to handle it," then the problem calls for 1/0 action. If, however, the individual lacks the capacity for handling the problem or if it overlaps the responsibilities of two people, it represents a 1/1 situation. If the problem is superordinate in the sense that each

FIGURE 7.1

CRITERIA	APPROACH		
	1/0 if	1/1 if	1/all if (1/some also)
1. Whose problem is it?	mine	his; both of us	ours
2. Time to contact	unavailable	available	available
3. Judgmental competence	full	low	insufficient
4. Pooling of information	unnecessary	vertical or horizontal	needed both horizontally and vertically
5. Synergy	not possible	possible	possible
6. Critique	no one else involved	problem belongs to two people	problem has implications for all
7. Significance to the team	low	low	high
8. Involvement-commitment of others	no significance	helpful-essential	necessary-essential
9. Relevance for others	none	present	present
10. Understanding by others of purpose or rationale of decision	no need can be assumed	needed	needed
11. Coordination of effort	unnecessary	vertical or horizontal	horizontal and vertical
12. Change in team norms/ standards	not relevant	not relevant	relevant
13. Representation of issue in other settings	none	pertinent	pertinent
14. Delegation	possible	unlikely	unlikely
15. Management development	none	present	present

individual has a piece of the problem but no one has all of it, then 1/all is the best interaction for solving it.

2 Time to Contact. If there is no time to involve others, for whatever sound reason, the individual takes the necessary action on a solo, or 1/0, basis. If consulting others will be advantageous and time is available to consult with one but not all, then it is a 1/1 situation. If time is available and there are advantages to several being involved, then it is 1/some of 1/all.

3 Judgmental Competence. A manager may have the depth and experience to exercise sound judgment. Other things equal, this is done in a 1/0 way. If the manager's experience in the field of a certain problem is insufficient, however, and one other person is needed to strengthen the soundness of judgment, the situation is 1/1. If reaching a sound judgment requires the participation of everyone, then it should be carried out in a 1/all team manner.

4 Pooling of Information. When all of the information needed to execute an action is possessed by one individual, 1/0 action is appropriate. If two people each have some of the information needed for the total understanding of a situation, then pooling of information may be required on a 1/1 basis. This may be a boss-subordinate relationship or it may be between equal-level colleagues. When all team members have unique aspects of information that need to be pooled to develop total comprehension, then 1/all pooling may be required.

5 Synergy. Teamwork may be desirable because of synergistic possibilities from several or all team members studying or reviewing a problem. The different perspectives team members apply to the problems and the clash of ideas that discussion can produce may result in a solution that is better in quality than any one, two, or several members might have developed. However, 1/0 is the rule if no synergy can be anticipated and 1/1 if only one other member can contribute.

6 Critique. Decision quality may be strengthened by discussions that study team skills in solving problems. If a problem has no team-building application, it should be studied in a 1/0 way by self-critique; in a 1/1 manner if two people can learn something about teamwork effectiveness from it; and in a 1/all way if the full team can benefit from studying it. In addition, there are many techniques of critique that aid team members to study results relative to performance. These are detailed elsewhere both in this book and others.[3]

The next criteria, numbers 7 through 13, are more closely related to the acceptance issue—i.e., the readiness of team members to implement a decision once it has been made.

7 Significance to the Team. If the action has no team implications beyond one member alone, unless he or she does not carry it out, it should be handled 1/0. If it has far-reaching operational significance, such as shifting the reporting lines in the organization, then the entire team should understand the issues. The greater the significance of an action for changing team purpose, direction, character, or procedures, the more desirable the participation and involvement of all members.

8 Involvement-Commitment of Others. Understanding of the problem and its solution may be necessary to achieve acceptance from those who must implement the decision. If the action to be taken does not involve other team members, it should be made 1/0. If it affects only one other, discussion with this team member is necessary (1/1). When the action has teamwide implications, all should discuss the pros and cons until those whose interests are involved have full understanding. Doubts and reservations are then relieved, and everyone is in a position of agreement and support.

9 Relevance for Others. Those whose future actions will be affected by a decision need to think through the issue and discuss its implications to see that it is understood and that they are committed to it. The larger the number of team members who have personal stakes in an action, the greater the need for them to discuss the decision.

10 Understanding by Others of Purpose or Rationale of Decision. There are some kinds of problems to which others cannot contribute, yet they can benefit from an awareness of the rationale employed in analyzing or solving it. When others already know the rationale or when it is not important to them, then the action should be 1/0. However, sometimes the rationale behind the action will benefit at least one other; therefore, it may need to be dealt with in a 1/1 way. All the others may not be in a position to contribute to a solution but may need to know the rationale, and under these circumstances the rationale should be communicated on a 1/all basis.

11 Coordination of Effort. Often an action can and should be 1/0 because there is no need for coordination. When coordination is required, the matter should be dealt with jointly, on a 1/1 basis. Sometimes several if not all team members are involved in implementing a decision; in that case the strategies for coordination need to be worked out on a 1/all basis.

12 Change in Team Norms/Standards. Norms/standards that influence performance on a within-team basis may need to be established, modified, or completely changed. All team members need to be involved for them to know and be committed to the new norms/standards. Because each team member adheres to team-based norms/standards, it is unlikely that a 1/0 action would be taken if it would shift a norm/standard. The most favorable condition for reaching such decisions is where a new team norm/standard is explicitly agreed to by all team members, particularly if the new norm/standard is intended to replace or modify an existing one.

13 Representation of Issue in Other Settings. Sometimes one team member serves as a representative in settings outside his or her own team situation. Other team members may contribute little or nothing to reaching a decision, but because they are in a "need to know" position, they are brought in to increase understanding.

These next two items are concerned specifically with using teamwork situations for management development.

14 Delegation. This arrangement is the opposite of 1/0, where the boss takes the problem and deals with it alone. This situation, expressed as 0/1, is a situation of complete delegation. A problem should be solved by a person of lesser rank if he or she has the understanding and judgment necessary to deal with it or if to do so would strengthen the subordinate's managerial effectiveness by increasing his or her capacity for exercising responsibility by taking on larger and larger problems. This shifts a 1/0 from one member to another. In addition, the boss is free to utilize this time on matters only he or she can solve.

A rule can be stated: other things being equal, 0/1 should be relied upon rather than 1/0 when (1) subordinates can deal with a given problem as well as or better than the boss; (2) the subordinate can strengthen managerial effectiveness; (3) delegation, not abdication, is the motivation that propels the boss in this direction; and (4) the time made available to the boss permits the solution of another problem more important than the delegated one, provided the conditions are such that the subordinate has reasonable prospects of success. Delegation is dealt with in more detail elsewhere.[4]

15 Management Development. Team members participate in analyzing managerial issues, even though they may have little to contribute to quality of management by way of information and even though their acceptance of it is immaterial. Their participation is to enable them to gain knowledge and to develop the judgment needed for dealing with such problems in the future. If a problem has no management development implications, then, other things being equal, it should be dealt with 1/0; if it has management development implications for only one other, it should be dealt with 1/1; if it has management development implications for all team members, it should be dealt with 1/all.

Grid Style Distortions of Teamwork

Sometimes people confuse "getting people together" or assembling people in the same physical location to engage in discussion with 9,9 teamwork. One way to examine this problem is to examine various Grid style distortions.

9,1

A manager with a 9,1 orientation is likely to hold periodic meetings that are justified in the following way:

> Accountability means that I am responsible for making decisions. Meetings are to communicate information or changes or to keep me abreast of work.

Managers with this orientation view decision making as the sole responsibility of the person who wears the highest cloak of authority. Information is gathered from lower levels to permit the best possible one-alone decisions. Even one-to-one decisions, where a subordinate participates in the decision-making process, are likely to be relatively rare. This does not mean that managers operating under a 9,1 orientation do not use meetings. They do, but the character of discussion gives a clue to the real reasons for meetings.

1,9

The manager with a 1,9 orientation is more likely to go overboard for groupness, not to achieve work purposes but to achieve sociability. Members of the group get together for the main purpose of sharing their thoughts. They share thoughts of a noncritical work nature and discuss some routine issues that arise and require attention. But a social relations motivation permeates many activities in the work situation, frequently under the guise of "consulting people to get their views."

As a result of the above, within a 1,9 work setting, the informal group flourishes. Each work nucleus has its own uniformity of opinions and attitudes about a wide range of matters. Conformity is valued to "get along well" and to be "liked by people." Deviation is likely to cause loss of acceptance.

5,5

Group sessions and special groups such as committees or task forces are relied on extensively. In this way, there is a heavy component of 1/all interaction with a 5,5 orientation. This manager says,

> I use a group meeting to give people a chance to participate. I am always open to suggestions. My group frequently makes recommendations that I give weight to in making the decision.

Committees serve several purposes. One is to give an opportunity for participation in discussions relevant to work without giving away authority. Another purpose is to avoid responsibility for and negative reactions from solo decisions in a subtle way. This can be done by basing them on group recommendations. A third way is more genuine. It is to elicit ideas and suggestions that can then be further evaluated for merit and possible use—and for personal credit.

1,1

In terms of meetings, the 1,1 orientation is "to hold regularly scheduled meetings, which are a matter of company policy." Obviously, the meetings are ones where decisions are not made but are simply communicated downward, as in the 9,1 example.

The concern of a manager whose characteristic style of management is 1,1 is turned inward. Only required production or social contact, which if ignored could place this manager's position in jeopardy, is maintained. Other events seem to pass unnoticed. Another way of picturing the 1,1 approach is in the "count me out" attitude. In the extreme, this manager often is able to find reasons for not attending department functions, informal meetings, or even regularly scheduled work meetings.

SUMMARY

These guidelines can be helpful to any manager in analyzing the organization of a 9,9-oriented team. They also can be useful in assisting managers to see opportunities for strengthening teamwork effectiveness.

Material in this chapter has been adapted from Robert R. Blake and Jane S. Mouton, *The New Managerial Grid* (Houston, Texas: Gulf Publishing Company, 1978), pp. 146–149.

8
Management-by-Objectives Through Goal Setting

Sound 9,9 management provides a basis for satisfying a person's need to contribute to the corporation. One point of application is learning to utilize management by objectives as the basis for personal involvement in forwarding the business. More significant and greater contributions are possible when managers are committed to achieving challenging goals than when their efforts are limited to completing day-by-day activities on a more or less stimulus/response basis. Aiding a subordinate to set goals for achievement that are within his or her power to reach calls for 9,9 versatility skills.

Conventional Approaches to Management-by-Objectives

Management-by-objectives is an approach that has enjoyed great popularity for many years. It is based on the notion that when people have objectives and have participated in setting them to some degree, the entire system of management is made more sensible, and people feel a greater sense of responsibility.

A management-by-objectives program is often brought into existence by top management's affirming the basic validity of the approach and authorizing its implementation. Implementation is through teaching managers a series of procedural steps, beginning with discussing objectives with a subordinate. Thereafter, these objectives are recorded and forwarded to a central office where they are accumulated and summarized. Sometimes program installers sit with the various groups to facilitate their understanding of what management-by-objectives requires, how to complete the written documents, and so on. This is a mechanical, tactical approach to management-by-objectives. It involves providing how-to-do-it instructions, forms, and other written support materials. Support may be provided by a facilitator who aids groups to walk through the various steps.

This approach can be compared with a strategic approach to management-by-objectives. A strategic approach does not begin with setting objectives but rather starts with the dynamics of goal setting. What is it about a goal that results in a person wanting to be involved and wanting to achieve it? There are many properties of goals that, if present, stimulate people to commit their energies to attaining that goal. Only when these properties arouse the involvement of those who must exert their energies to achieve them are there likely to be meaningful results from a program involving management-by-objectives.

Thus we see the strategic importance of first understanding the human dynamics of involvement in goals, before getting down to concrete objectives. When a strategy of goal setting is not set before entering into the tactics, the "commitments" that a person makes under a conventional management-by-objectives program will diminish and disappear almost as soon as the boss turns his or her head.

Behavioral science research has identified a number of properties that a goal must have if it is to stimulate effort.

Motivational Dynamics of Goals

Personal "Ownership"

Of singular importance for effective management-by-objectives through goal setting is the concept of ownership. People are motivated most to reach a goal when it "belongs" to them. Then they are involved and become committed to reaching it.

Ownership does not come from being given a goal in the following ways:

- "Do it!"
- "Would you please?"
- "Do it or not if you want."
- "Why not take a shot at it?"

The 9,9 alternative is that a person considers all aspects of a goal and, in doing so, becomes involved in the possibility of really being successful in reaching it. The final aspect of "ownership" is shown when a person gives his or her personal commitment to the challenge. Then the individual has taken it inside; the individual now "owns" it. All of the following contribute to ownership.

Clarity

An essential attribute of a goal is that it be clear to the person responsible for reaching it. A goal may be well understood by a boss who believes adequate directions for accomplishing it have been given, but what is wanted may still be unclear to the subordinate. When this is the case, the subordinate is unable to decide on what action he or she has to take or to join efforts with others to accomplish the goal in a meaningful way. Yet when a subordinate is clear as to what the goal is and what is entailed in achieving it, effort can be put into reaching it.

Meaningfulness

Sometimes an activity is a meaningful, coherent unit. All components fit together, making a sensible whole. At other times the same activity is fragmented into "mechanical" pieces, and the pieces do not have any inherent meaning to the person responsible for performing the activity. The pieces by themselves are unlikely to make sense. Whether or not the activity is a meaningful whole in itself is an important factor in a successful effort. In setting goals if the goal is an arbitrary fragment of something larger, it is less likely to be motivating than if it is a functional whole, a unit unto itself. This kind of goal gives the person responsible for achieving it a sense of completeness when the goal is reached.

Significance

A goal may be clear and it may be a meaningful whole, and yet it may not be regarded as important. It may be so trivial as to produce an attitude of "So what?" A goal is only likely to be motivating if it is of a significant nature. Possessing significance, then, is an important property of a goal, even though any isolated part in and of itself may not be "important." An example is the spare tire. If never used, it is not important to have one. However, at a distance of 35 or 40 miles from a telephone a blowout makes the spare tire highly relevant. There are many such examples in daily living.

Difficulty (Remoteness)

Another property that contributes to the motivational character of a goal is its degree of difficulty. A goal that can be accomplished with little effort is not likely to be motivating. Stacking a dishwasher with two place settings day in and day out is unlikely to be challenging. Although necessary, it presents a person with little excitement. At the other extreme, a goal so difficult as to create a high probability of failure is also unlikely to be motivating.

Thus it becomes important to set goals within these limitations. Even difficult-to-achieve goals can be set that are realistic as long as the assessment of the effort needed to reach them is accurate, given reasonable opportunity.

Sometimes a goal that is very difficult can become motivating when its components can be dealt with as subgoals, so that the main, difficult goal is achievable a step at a time. Getting a college degree can be seen as a very difficult or remote goal to a freshman, but completing the freshman year as a subgoal can be challenging.

The Time Between Goal Setting and Goal Reaching

A goal can be too remote, in the sense of being projected so far into the future that it is unrealistic for an individual to feel urgency, immediateness, or relevance in efforts to achieve it. As a result, goals that can only be reached in the longer term are unlikely to be very motivating, unless they, too, can be divided into a series of subgoals, each of which is meaningful and attainable within a reasonable period of time.

By the same line of reasoning, a goal that can be attained almost immediately or in the near term is unlikely to be challenging. The reason is that a near-term goal that is easy to reach does not "test" a person; it poses no challenge. Even though value might be associated with achieving it, it does not stimulate the kind of involvement and effort that a more difficult goal might promote.

From a time perspective point of view, the "ideal" goal is one that is not located so far in the future as to be out of sight and yet is not so close in time as to be too easy to attain. It needs to be located far enough in the future to make reaching the goal feasible, yet not be so far away that the sense of urgency is lost.

Zeigarnik Effect

Another characteristic of a goal is called the Zeigarnik or "completion" effect, named after the German scientist who studied it. The idea is this. Once an individual feels ownership or personal commitment, efforts to reach the goal give rise to internal tensions that push for a successful outcome. If barriers are encountered that block goal achievement, the person is unlikely to say, "I got blocked." Rather, the individual increases efforts to remove the barrier. These internal tensions constitute an aspect of motivation. They help to account for why committed people do not quit simply because difficulties are encountered.

Feedback

Feedback tells an individual what progress is being made toward the goal. Measurements and other indicators furnish the necessary information for knowing whether performance is on track and on time. Feedback provides an indication of whether or not actions are appropriate in relation to what needs to be done. Without feedback a person is "flying blind," and the motivation to continue is much lower than it is if feedback is available. As an example, many companies assess progress through a financial year in terms of quarters, months, or weeks. In this way, information is always at hand about whether the objectives for a given financial period are being met. If they are not, changes can be introduced.

Another example of a feedback loop is in the health area. A person, for example, sets a goal of losing weight, desiring to reduce his weight of 220 pounds to 154. The time frame is a 12-month period. If such a self-management-by-objectives approach is consistent with other aspects described, a person may employ feedback by first plotting the amount of weight reduction to be accomplished during each week from beginning to end. This can be done based on verified trends of weight reduction. In the beginning of the program, dieters can expect to lose more each week or each day than they are likely to lose in the same period as the final objective approaches. Feedback is provided as to whether performance is satisfactory or whether different effort is essential to realize the objective. The motivating effects are lost without daily or weekly feedback. Weekly feedback tends to be the more motivating of the two because daily eating behavior is more difficult to relate to its cumulative impact on weight reduction.

Operational goals can be stated in many different ways. Some of these involve financial statements. Yet operational statements often are better because they fit actually more closely. For example, an on-time airline is one that satisfies customers' needs better than an airline that performs poorly in this regard. The airline can set a goal of, for example, 90% on-time departures and arrivals to be reached over a three- or six-month period. It can then continuously study actual performance to see if it is moving in the direction required to meet the objective as established. With knowledge of whether progress is or is not being made, it becomes possible to evaluate whether additional steps are needed. If they are, what is required to implement these steps can be determined. Without the use of actual performance as feedback, less progress toward the objective is to be expected than when accurate and frequent feedback is available.

Some kinds of work cannot provide direct feedback. For example, a pharmaceuticals detailer does not take orders, even though he or she brings various drugs and chemical agents to the attention of physicians. The detailer demonstrates the availability of these pharmaceuticals and then focuses discussion on their effects and value. Since no order is taken from the doctor, there is no immediate or direct way of knowing whether the effort expended is moving toward the goal of increasing company sales. In this case an indirect feedback is needed and can be obtained by monitoring orders placed by pharmacists and hospitals, these being the "sales outlets" and the doctor an extension of the drug company's marketing arm.

The Goal Gradient

An interesting property of a goal involves what is known as the goal gradient and the effects this gradient exerts on behavior. The idea is that one becomes more and more involved in achieving a goal the closer one gets ot its completion. While understandable, this property of a goal can produce very undesirable side effects.

An example will illustrate the problem. Attempts to escape from prison become far more frequent the closer the prisoner comes to completing the prison term and being released. The goal of freedom becomes so compelling that the prisoner "can't wait," and so he or she does the very thing that prolongs imprisonment. Animals reveal the same behavior. Rats, for example, in running a maze, have more difficulty eliminating "mistakes" the closer they come to the feedbox.

Another example of what happens from the standpoint of the goal gradient aspect of goal setting is referred to as the Stackhanoff effect, named after a Russian. It identifies a characteristic of behavior first observed in Soviet factories. What happens is that a goal, really an objective that is expressed as a quota, is established for how much of a product is to be produced in a month. At the beginning of the month work is slow and carried out in a leisurely way. Productivity remains low, and this may continue through the first twenty or more days of the month. Everyone realizes that the quota will not be reached unless a "total" effort is put forth. Thus, the Stackhanoff effect. In the last few days of the month, stupendous effort is expended and the quota reached. Needless to say, at the beginning of the next month people are exhausted from the "total" effort, and it is understandable why work slows down and a leisurely pace is resumed, until the same dilemma is faced at the end of the next month.

The obvious solution is to understand the dynamic involved. By getting true involvement in the objective it becomes possible to manage the pace of work, insuring that work is not so hard as to be exhausting at any point along the road to the goal. When effort is maintained at the highest attainable level the finding is that total output is increased, even above the ceiling set by the quota.

The Stackhanoff effect is actually much more widespread than might be realized. For example, taking a leisurely attitude toward study in the beginning of a college term and then cramming at the end to get a "B" in the final exam is the same phenomenon. Christmas shopping on December 24 and completing and mailing one's income tax at midnight on April 15 are other examples.

This phenomenon explains why labor-management negotiations sometimes break down just before contract signing. If either union or management becomes overeager for success and thinks the outcome is in the bag, last-minute demands may be made that are unacceptable. Similar examples can be found in various commercial negotiations.

Hierarchy of Goals

Two or more goals may be established, but without awareness that they are mutually incompatible. Take the instance of two positive objectives, both of which are equally attractive. One involves funding R&D to be in a stronger competitive position in the long term. Another is to use the same funds for launching a new product that will add to the product line. Funds are insufficient to do both, and a splitting of funds may well mean that neither is done well enough to make a significant difference. Under these conditions there is no basis for establishing priority; therefore, neither action can be successfully undertaken.

Managers often face goals of equal value that are incompatible with one another, with no criteria to resolve the impasse. The solution is that issues of priority be dealt with and resolved in the process of goal setting in terms of a "hierarchy of goals." This is in contrast to establishing a number of goals without considering the possibility that they may be incompatible and that the actions taken to serve one goal will necessarily work against the actions needed to serve another.

If this had been done in the case above, a manager at some level would take responsibility for establishing a priority of hierarchy of goals between the long-term R&D goals or the short-term product line enlargement goal.

One of the most common sources of incompatibility among goals relates to getting people involved in and feeling responsible for long-range planning while at the same time getting them involved in and feeling responsible for strengthening short-term results. Both of these are highly attractive goals, and yet we know that long-range planning is routinely sacrificed when these two goals enjoy equally high priority.

It is possible to solve the incompatibility in any number of ways. One is by delegation of responsibility for short-term results to others, and in this way gaining the time necessary for long-range planning. Another is by manning. If delegation of responsibility is impossible and time is insufficient to effectively do both, the solution may call for a manning decision that permits effective delegation to occur. A third solution is appropriate in some situations. That is, simply to cut down the amount of work done inside the organization itself through contracting work or services. Results may be gained in this indirect manner, and the time needed for effective long-range planning will thus be made available.

There are many ways of setting priorities among equally attractive goals. These examples demonstrate constructive solutions that are possible once the hierarchy of goals issue itself becomes clear. Then managers can take the initiative to assign priorities to goals and in this way create the conditions under which those that are agreed to can be achieved.

Involvement, Participation, and Commitment: The Goal-Setting Ingredients of 9,9 Versatility

Management-by-objectives through goal setting rests for its motivation on the active involvement of those engaged in supervising and implementing the goals. The benefits of shared participation include the following.

- Thinking through goals that one may become responsible for implementing provides an individual basis of personal understanding and insight and, therefore, of improved self-direction.
- Thinking through goals stimulates involvement in the real issues, arousing commitment to success.
- Only by open and shared boss/subordinate participation, which recognizes that both boss and subordinate inevitably have a role in doing the things needed to achieve a goal and that one cannot act without the other, does it become possible to avoid the risks inherent in other possible approaches.

1. A boss who imposes objectives on a subordinate by relying on a 9,1 orientation is likely to arouse apparent compliance but inner resentment that, even though unexpressed, serves to undermine the entire effort.

2. A person who sets goals in a management-by-objectives context in a 1,9 way is likely to "follow" the subordinate's wishes rather than to confront the real thinking about excellence. This will result in the setting of limited goals.

3. Only mediocre results can be anticipated from a management-by-objectives program in the 5,5 context because the manager seeks to adjust and accommodate to subordinates' views in ways that will result in increasing the boss's popularity with subordinates.

4. The 1,1 approach is so minimal with regard to shared participation that it permits little more than lip service.

A 9,9-oriented boss who values and works for the participation of subordinates, is alert to their reservations and doubts, and deals with them through insight-based resolution, is likely to earn their commitment to achieving goals. When these conditions prevail, management-by-objectives through a goal-setting program can make significant contributions to organization success, operationally and through real development of its people.

How to Do It

Several steps are involved in using goal setting as a 9,9 versatility skill.

Start by Identifying Goals, Not by Dealing with Current Problems

One place to start is at the other end from the "here-and-now." The "other end" is defined by what might be achieved. Identifying achievements is the initial step in the formulization of goals.

The best approach to identifying conditions at the "other end" is found by thinking through "ideal" outcomes, which is to say soundest outcomes, not idealistic ones, as contrasted with what might at the moment appear practical and "realistic." By thinking in terms of such ideal possibilities and imagining what the situation will be when goals are successfully achieved, opportunities are spotted that might otherwise go unrecognized. If these opportunities are not identified, they can have no influence on behavior nor can they supply a rationale for change. Lacking those positive motivating forces, managers are left with only a narrow, short-term, stimulus-response perspective, rather than a vision of what is truly possible.

Several sources of data to stimulate thinking about ideal possibilities can be consulted.

- Conclusions about desirable outcomes reached in a previously completed performance appraisal and review
- The boss's own perceptions of the areas where a subordinate's performance needs improvement and of opportunities the subordinate may be unaware of
- Review of individual job descriptions in comparison with present performance may point to goals needing to be achieved
- Grid seminar summaries from Friday activities can supply important clues as to areas of performance where significant improvement is needed
- Team building as part of organization development, which often results in specific improvement goals being identified

Obviously not all "ideal" formulations are achievable. Sometimes, after an "ideal" goal has been identified and the specific and concrete steps necessary to reach it have been evaluated, it is no longer seen as realistic; it is recognized to be impractical. Then it may be necessary to abandon the goal or to pare it down to some lesser objective that can be accomplished. Absence of testing against the reality factor is what causes ideal thinking to become and to be seen as *idealistic* and to cease having force in influencing behavior.

Walking Backwards into the Here-and-Now

The next step is to walk backwards from the goal as stated and to identify the concrete steps necessary to realize the objectives. Those engaged in the activity can simulate, rehearse, or otherwise test their proposed steps as the actual, concrete, specific steps to be taken prior to finalizing them.

The advantage of making this evaluation is that barriers that might otherwise loom unexpectedly and insurmountably can be anticipated and dealt with in a problem-solving manner. Another benefit is that the activity results in designing an operational plan that becomes a working blueprint for future action.

Characterizing the Here-and-Now

From a walking-backwards point of view, the last step is to specify in an objective way what the prevailing here-and-now conditions are. Does the here and now contain obstacles that will block goal achievement? If so, these must be resolved. In any event, analyzing the actual situation in detail provides a realistic picture of the starting situation. Then the situation is set up for managing by objectives through goal setting.

Implementing the Management-by-Objectives Action Plan

Once identified and established, the activity shifts into an agreed-upon management-by-objectives action program. Managing the implementation of these objectives, through a sound mix of supervision, consultation, resourcing, and self-direction, is the final step. This is facilitated by drawing up a written plan of action through which the objectives are to be achieved. Specific steps to be taken are scheduled against time requirements. Critique points are designated for review of progress against objectives with replanning sequences built in to provide for unforeseen circumstances and changes in conditions.

The "Paper" Program of Mechanics

Once managers expend this kind of effort in setting ideal/optimal goals, rehearsing the success dynamics that achievement is expected to release, and specifying the action program for realization, a "paper" program for control of the process is no longer essential. The "paper," desirable for keeping the overall effort in clear focus, then comes to be seen as a support for the activity rather than as a burden that is irrelevant, resented, and resisted when the motivational underpinnings of a truly sound goal-setting activity are not truly present.

The basic principle of behavior introduced earlier is that "activity carried out within a framework of goals and objectives is a better basis for committed self-direction than is direction from the outside." Evidence was presented for the importance of goals in organizing human activity and harnessing human motivations to purposeful outcomes. Nothing is more frustrating and boredom-producing than activities that are continuous but never reach an end or a goal, such as assembly-line operations or random activities that do not add up. By comparison, activities that (1) have a purpose, (2) challenge a person's self-worth, and (3) permit a person to feel that he or she is making an important contribution stimulate rather than frustrate.

The versatility aspect can be seen in several ways. It has been shown that families that have goals actually rear children who are stronger and more effective in attaining autonomy than are children from families in which family goals are weak, absent, or imposed. Youngsters who set goals that involve earning money, achieving the kind of scholastic performance they feel the challenge to reach, and achieving the career they hope to enter, are mentally and emotionally healthier and more in control of themselves than are those who do not set goals. Workers and managers respond more favorably to the opportunity of contribution when their work is formulated in terms of goals and objectives and when specific activities add up to and result in the achievement of meaningful end results.

Learning to set goals for oneself and learning to help others set goals is one aspect of the versatility requirement. Gaining commitment is another essential component. The skills essential for bringing about shared participation and commitment based on understanding and agreement are essential for introducing management-by-objectives through goal setting.

How Management-by-Objectives through Goal Setting Relates to 9,9 Versatility

Another versatility aspect lies in being able to conceive in imagination what might truly be possible. To do so it is necessary to separate oneself from those blinding influences that often arise from existing circumstances.

In this connection, standards for deciding "How good is good?" are needed, and in managing-by-objectives through goal setting, the best standard is *excellence*. There are several ways to define excellence. "If that goal were to be reached, the problem would be solved once and for all" is one way. "That reflects the true solution" is another. "This is the most that can be realized under the realistic competition we face" is a third way to get a sense of what would be "excellent." Another way of characterizing excellence is to say what it is not: "That would be better than last year," or "We'd better cut down on that because you can never predict what will happen." Excellence, in other words, is the best that rigorous thinking and analysis can visualize.

Often goals based on excellence are really no more difficult and far more rewarding to reach than are others based on convention or mediocrity. The difference is in their quality, which, in itself, is an important source of motivation for extra effort.

SUMMARY

There is a widespread need for goals that give direction, stimulate effort, and give work a meaningful character in the pursuit of personal and organizational excellence. Goal setting is a way of identifying and getting involved in reaching some objective. Being able to foresee a goal makes it possible to set a sequence for the explicit steps necessary for getting to the goal in an orderly, economical way. The likelihood of getting there is increased when steps are identified, agreed to in advance, and set in a flexible way so they can be changed as the situation itself changes. The route to achieving a goal should be thoroughly outlined, with specific steps formulated by the persons responsible for taking them to gain the advantages of involvement and commitment to their implementation.

A management-by-objectives approach is doomed to failure if it disregards these properties of goals and proceeds in a mechanical, paper-controlled manner. The reason is that the motivating value that comes from involvement is absent. Therefore managerial behavior is influenced very little. The potential rewards made possible when people are committed to sound goals and objectives are lost both to the individual and to the organization as a whole.

9

Using Organization Rewards to Motivate Productivity

Fulfillment through contribution is the 9,9 motivation for changing things to make them better or more productive. How would a company that desires to stimulate managers to develop such versatility skills use the reward system for doing so? This is an all-important question. The underlying rationale is that, by and large, managers tend to do the things they are rewarded for and to avoid doing things that are ignored or punished.

Even though organizations reward employees, the rewards may not be very closely related to contribution. Therefore, we need to understand several things about personal motivations and organization rewards. One is to be aware of the different motivations of individual employees, from janitor to executive. The second is to become more aware of the different kinds of rewards that organizations offer their employees. Finally, we need to know how these are interrelated. Only when an organization rewards employees for bringing about needed changes can we expect efforts toward corporate excellence to be stimulated. When such efforts are rewarded, the individual is likely to feel personal fulfillment resulting from his or her contribution.

Organization Rewards

From a corporate point of view, wide agreement exists on the just basis of rewarding performance. The just way is when reward is based on merit. The idea is that people who contribute more than their colleagues are moving the corporation forward more. Because they are doing so, greater benefits from the standpoint of organization rewards should come their way. This is reward based on merit. Merit implies that what people do can be weighed and evaluated as to who contributes more and who contributes less along a continuum, like a ruler or a yardstick. The weighing scale includes immediate results achieved; other positive corporate benefits, such as reduced expense of production; and long-term implications for the organization's future effectiveness, such as using work as the basis for developing subordinates and the organization.

There are many examples of how a contribution to the organization's future effectiveness is acknowledged. In science, merit is evaluated in terms of basic discoveries, their consequences for new discoveries, and their implications for the future of science and the human race. Honors are bestowed on those whose discoveries permit new developments beyond possibilities previously realized or solve fundamental human problems of health, safety, development, or happiness. The Nobel prize is an example of rewarding merit for outstanding contributions to science, medicine, and peace. Those judged to have made the most outstanding contributions to literature receive the Pulitzer prize. Contributions to film making and acting are recognized by the highly prized Oscars. The same is true in sports. Players judged to have made the greatest impact in terms of success of the team and teamwork are singled out for public recognition, as in the case of the Heisman Trophy in the United States and comparable awards elsewhere. In many spheres of activity, personal merit based on contribution is acknowledged through organization rewards that are both symbolic and financial.

These are, of course, cases involving contributions that are highly visible and truly exceptional. The question is, can we expect the same respect for merit in business and industry, where people are engaged in less visible and more corporately interrelated sets of activities? In government and service institutions, such as health delivery systems?

Many organizations are geared to rewarding the most meritorious contribution the most highly, and so on, down to the other end of the scale, where those who have blocked or hampered results are dismissed or penalized. From a motivational point of view, it is a valid premise to offer the greatest reward for the most outstanding contribution. This means that through applying talent, the person rewarded most is adding most to the products or services an organization makes available to society in its pursuit of achievement, comfort, satisfaction, and happiness.

The first proposition is: the larger the personal contribution and the greater the promise of further improvement the larger the reward offered.

The second proposition is: financial rewards are personally motivating to those who do most to advance corporate success. Because of the greater responsibility they shoulder and, therefore, the greater contribution they can make, those who lead the most financially successful corporations generally receive the greatest reward. This is not to say that all rewards are financial in character, and a tax system may result in perquisites that are more valuable than their equivalents in money. The tactics change, not strategy.

Motivation of Individuals

Now we turn the question around and ask, "How does motivation look from the viewpoint of the person whose performance is under evaluation by the system?"

Research is a basic necessity for answering this. The most critical factor from which people derive satisfaction is doing a challenging job well and being rewarded for it. Unfortunately work that is inherently stimulating may not be the same work that an organization needs to have done. When an individual is asked to perform unstimulating but necessary work, individual and organizational goals are far apart. Even here, however, when employees are committed to the organization's success, work not interesting may come to motivate. When there are jobs that cannot be regarded as containing any genuine emotional appeal, ingenuity is applied to find ways to automate or eliminate them.

Thus, while the aim may be for all work to be inherently meaningful and for an organization not to need any other kind of work, the possibility of achieving this aim is wholly unreal. Nevertheless, this disability in no way diminishes the importance of rewarding contribution based upon merit.

Motivations other than contribution are present in organizations today, even though merit might still be relied upon as the key measure for reward. Each of these motivations may be important in "telling" a manager what to do to get rewarded.

Is Rewarding Contribution Based on Merit the Sole Factor in Motivation?

9,1-Oriented Motivation

9,1-oriented efforts involve a person in seeking to dominate, master, and control a situation for which he or she is responsible. This personal motivation may cause the fittest to survive and the weak or incompetent to fall by the wayside. If, at the same time, the best come to the top, the corporation will survive; if not, it, too, will fall by the wayside. Thus, even though this kind of personal motivation may at times serve organization goals, side effects that are adverse to total organization effectiveness also can result.

One of these side effects is to influence performance by punishing failure to perform up to standards. The reasoning is that punishment is painful, with the result that people will do whatever is necessary to avoid incurring pain. This thesis is basic to the authority-obedience concept of control, which is inherent to a 9,1 orientation. In addition to using punishment to create pressure for performance, the 9,1 concept includes the idea that obedience is rewarded. Rewards, however, are kept to a minimum since obedience is expected and rewards are used only when necessary. The use of reward and punishment in this way may or may not be related to merit. Indeed, it is most likely to be related to a boss's desire to ensure that his or her directions are carried out in the ways specified.

A study of managers and workers provides a perspective on the 9,1 orientation that pits person against person.[5] It produces antagonism, resentment, rebelliousness, fighting back, and antiorganizational creativity. The side effects from slowdown, working to rule, strikes, and so on, indicate that a 9,1 approach to rewarding performance suffers such expensive consequences as to be intolerable.

1,9-Oriented Motivation

Another idea is that performance can be influenced in a plus direction by personal rewards, as contrasted with reward based on compensation. Thus the manager is advised to "stroke" subordinates, that is, to compliment them by reacting appreciatively when subordinates do what is wanted. The concept is that strokes are interpreted as 1,9-oriented acceptance. In this context it is likely that a minus motivation is avoided when something undesirable is done. Rather, when mistakes occur they are expected to disappear by virtue of being ignored. This is the 1,9 orientation to "psychic" compensation.

Seeking to create and maintain a stable organization by strengthening loyalty and cooperation is another 1,9 approach to linking organization rewards to individual motivation. This is done by providing people with a pleasing visual environment of color, design, and decoration; providing entertainment through piped music; providing a coffee lounge, carpets on the floor, and so on. This 1,9 orientation to motivation is geared to keeping people happy and comfortable. Reducing complaints by eliminating outer symptoms that cause these complaints, rather than stimulating involvement and participation in promoting the corporation's real effectiveness is the distinctive feature. Satisfying these kinds of often legitimate needs is basic in the sense that failure to do so is out of tune with the times and constitutes deprivation. But as organization rewards for loyalty and cooperation, these rarely motivate contribution.

5,5-Oriented Motivation

Another motivation involves rewarding popularity.

Promotions indicate who has the most prestige. It is the popular person who knows how to get attention, to be seen, and to be noticed when this is what gets rewarded. This is a 5,5 orientation to rewarding "effort." The appropriate actions frequently include dressing well, knowing the rules of social decorum, giving the "right" person needed support, having the right sponsor, and the like. Unfortunately, these sources of popularity rarely stimulate managers to take the kinds of actions that contribute to organization success. One's own success in being popular comes first, regardless of whether or not the organization benefits from that popularity. There is little evidence that organizations do benefit from it.

1,1-Oriented Motivation

Some reward systems are based on seniority. The oldest person in years of service gets the most—the most pay and the longest vacations. This individual is the last to be laid off in periods of adversity. This is a 1,1 orientation to motivation. It is unrelated to production and makes no distinction between individuals in terms of differences in their contributions. Length of service, even of "hanging on," is the criterion. Rewarding lengthy service rather than the quality or character of service may be adverse to productivity, as is seen in the following.

The U.S. Civil Service system gives an example of seniority and its key significance. In designing a rewards system so as to acknowledge merit, the following is reported.

> Treasury Department public-information officer William
> F. Rhatican sought to cut his overstaffed office: "I had
> 30 people doing a job that could have been accomplished
> by 10." After six months Rhatican abandoned his effort.
> Under Civil Service regulations, "the proposed smaller
> office would have to be staffed not by the ten most
> competent but by the ten most senior," he explained.[6]

In addition to the key role in reward for seniority, an additional problem is that administrators have lost control of three basic managerial tools—the power to hire, to demote, and to fire.

> A manager must be prepared to spend up to one half of his time for 6 to 18 months to remove one Civil Service employe. Most simply refuse. Many choose to "work around" an incompetent employe or "Kick him upstairs." Others fake a good performance rating for a troublesome worker and recommend him to others, to get rid of him.[7]

An example of the relation between productivity and seniority from a Department of Agriculture memo requesting a crackdown on "significant problems of attendance" follows:

> Employes were warned against the "poor image" conveyed by "tardiness, eating breakfast immediately after reporting for work, extended coffee breaks, excessive lunch periods and early departures." But any results are non-apparent. In the elevator an employe tells a companion, "I'd like to be sick tomorrow, but I can't. The woman I work with plans to be."[8]

Of course, it is not that firing is impossible; it is only that a gigantic appeal process has been created that practically ensures employment continuity.

In summing this up, Mortimer Caplin, chairman of the National Civil Service League and former Internal Revenue Service commissioner, said:

> We need a recommitment to the principles and practice of merit in public employment.[9]

This amounts to a massive bureaucratic bypass of the original concept inherent in Civil Service, in which managers were freed from the old "spoils system" so that they could operate their departments according to a "merit system." What this fail-safe system of employment produces is something close to "absolute" security reminiscent of the tenure system in universities.

In addition to the symptoms already mentioned, the consequences of this kind of system are evident everywhere.

Yet substantial movement away from a merit system already has occurred in the institutions of commerce and industry. This is partly related to union clauses as they apply to hiring and firing employees. Also, in managerial ranks there is a subtle, 5,5-oriented way of conceiving the problem. No individual wants to be conspicuous by taking actions against a person of subordinate rank for fear that by doing so popularity will be reduced. Additionally, the security of "team" membership may be sacrificed. Add to this the fact that, in many large corporations, no boss, acting alone, can bring about a dismissal but must clear any such action with a boss one, two, and sometimes more than two levels up. Thus it is evident that in many ways significant aspects of a seniority system are already accepted in industry.

Other Motivational Systems

Another major option for organization of a reward system is the communist one: from each according to ability, to each according to need. This formulation splits contribution from reward. It does so on the assumption that a person of greater talent will apply it spontaneously, even though no material recognition of it is given by way of acknowledgment or appreciation. It is the same the other way around: whatever people need in material terms is provided without regard to the quality or quantity of their contribution. This concept that effort is made spontaneously does not square with the facts of human motivation, where the desire for personal gain related to effort is a self-evident factor in stimulating contribution.

Contribution is undoubtedly the most valid basis of organization reward in modern industrial systems, not only from a private or personal point of view, but from the standpoint of organization success.

The Organization's Goal in Rewarding Performance

Organizations might wisely seek to shift the attitudes and emotions of those employed by them toward the 9,9 orientation. A key way of doing so is by ensuring that the reward system most benefits those whose contributions make the most difference to the corporation's success, both short and long term.

The question then is, "What should be avoided in a reward system and how is it done?"

What to Avoid in a Reward System

First and foremost are across-the-board raises. This treats everyone alike, and the justification usually is "no one is treated unfairly." Actually the opposite is true. Those making the greatest contributions are brought to the same level as those who have contributed the least. This means that the best contributors are receiving far less benefit from their contributions than are those who contribute least.

Another practice to be avoided is the idea that small differences that distinguish one individual's contribution from another, even though they remain in the same relative positions, make little or no difference. Nothing could be farther from the truth. What people judge is amount of change relative to their colleagues. If X gets a salary change of $500 and Y of $550, not the $500 but the $50 difference is the basis of comparison. Such a difference will be resented if it can be justified only by seniority, friendship, popularity, or slavish devotion, rather than by contribution. The research on relative deprivation, conducted during World War II, was conclusive in demonstrating the validity of these propositions.

A final factor to be avoided is secrecy. The silence factor in most compensation programs is interrupted at only two points. One is principal officers' compensation reported publicly in corporate annual reports. The other is union contracts, often specifying pay level by job classification and spelling out overtime payment. These two exceptions are brought about by legal considerations rather than corporate commitment to an open payment system. All other aspects of payment are most likely to be silent or secret.

It can be accepted that something so widespread as the silence that presently exists about salary treatment has come into being for specific reasons. The most obvious is to hide the perceived inequity that often results when one is aware of what one's colleagues earn in comparison with oneself. There are likely to be discrepancies between an individual's idea and his or her superior's idea of that individual's worth to the corporation relative to others'. Many managers believe that these kinds of discrepancies provoke feelings of antagonism, jealousy, envy, and so on, which disrupt smooth performance. The rationale is that by keeping these differences private, it is possible to avoid adverse emotional attitudes.

Is it true that subordinates' seniors can evaluate contribution more objectively than the contributors themselves? Probably partly so, as evaluating one's own or others' contributions is subject to self-deception. These comparisons are affected by vested interests. Yet, on the other hand, many factors, such as like or dislike, influence how persons are evaluated by their seniors. These subjective factors, although used, are not related to contribution.

The most equitable system is when seniors make judgments that are open and therefore subject to correction when inequities are demonstrated. Such a system puts a premium on high-quality performance appraisals that aid a person to be self-objective and to identify factors that can be changed, which, if changed, would result in revised estimates of the individual's worth in the organization.

The above are indicators of what to avoid. They are important, but the real question is, "What to do?"

What to Do

Objective criteria which will relate personal reward to profit contribution should be used whenever possible. This is one of the motivations behind the trend of the sixties that led to dividing the overall business structure into subunits that could be evaluated. This division allows measurable expenses to be weighed against comparable contributions from each unit. Thereafter, compensation can be related to the value obtained from the effort invested. This is a positive approach, except when it results in cutting corners on quality, management development, and so on. These shortcuts may not adversely affect long-term results for some time, but when they do, the losses, monetary and otherwise, can be substantial.

Another involves "opening" the reward system to public review. This step is strongly resisted, as previously discussed. The reasons are that inequities are now public knowledge, and previously hidden differences can provoke deep resentments. Nevertheless, an open reward system is valuable because it clearly focuses on the need to face up to and resolve inequities.

A third is to ensure that differential treatment is based on two criteria: (1) the worth of a person's efforts in furthering corporate effectiveness, and (2) comparative judgments of contributions by those who perform in the same area under comparable opportunities. This person-to-person comparison is basic. It should be made explicit because those who are judged also compare themselves with one another in this way. Only with such comparisons is it possible for those who evaluate contribution to do so against a standard of "more or less."

Still another consideration in evaluation is a person's potential relative to future, in contrast with current performance. This can be seen by asking the question, "Of two runners both doing the 100-yard dash, with one at his maximum here-and-now time of 10 seconds, and the other potentially capable of getting to 9 seconds, which should get the greatest encouragement and the best coaching?"

The same question can be posed in management. Of two employees contributing equally at a given point in time, greater opportunity should be awarded to the one with the greatest potential. Otherwise, this employee is likely to disregard the importance of developing potential because it is "unimportant" or may seek employment elsewhere where greater appreciation of his or her potential is present.

SUMMARY

Since people tend to do the things for which they are rewarded and to avoid what is not rewarded or what is punished, it is important to gear the organization's reward system to the 9,9 fulfillment of the organization's real needs through contribution. Outside the 9,9 orientation of managing, this is not the dominating motivation. More often it is that of beating others in a 9,1 orientation of blind ambition; staying on "the right side" of people, the 5,5 orientation; acting to gain the approval of others, which is the 1,9 orientation; or simply seeking to hang on until retirement, which is the perspective of 1,1.

When organizations treat contribution as a primary and essential need, then it is unnecessary to resort to using seniority as the basis of reward, prestige as the basis of promotion, across-the-board raises, and keeping people in the same position relative to one another. Merit-based contribution is best utilized as the basis of a reward system when effort is subject to objective measurement through profit, cost, or contribution criteria; when an "open" system of payment is maintained; when judgments involve person-to-person comparisons; and when potential is assessed, understood, and acknowledged.

10
9,9 Team Learning from Experience Through Critique

Academic learning, demonstration projects, and critique are three important ways of acquiring insight and understanding. Of these three, critique is the most pertinent for aiding a manager to increase personal effectiveness by learning from experience.

Critique involves evaluating action in a thoughtful way before the action is taken, during the action itself, and when it has been completed. It is important because the tests of soundness of planning lie in the results achieved and in the explanations of the reasons why the results are what they are. Critique establishes these explanations. Better understanding through critique of the cause-and-effect actions that result in solving a given problem is thus the key to better planning for improved results in dealing with similar problems in the future.

Academic learning, where an individual needs to understand the logic and feelings of another through books, lectures, movies, and so on, is a powerful tool promoting improved human understanding. It is frequently carried out in a manner that is not very stimulating and is often quite boring. Nonetheless, it is a relatively efficient way of transmitting ideas from someone who understands them to others who do not. In this way, a transfer of knowledge is attained. Often, the kinds of learning undertaken in an academic environment leave it to the individual to grapple with the translation of concepts into practice. This is even true in university education. The case-study method is an example of aiding individuals to acquire understanding, but the problem of practical application is left primarily to the student.

Academic learning of the sort described here is not learning from experience. It is not critique because individuals are not engaged in studying their own specific circumstances to learn from these circumstances how to change them.

Another method of learning that does not involve critique in any rigorous sense of the word is the demonstration project. Demonstration projects have in recent times become a preferred way of introducing new methods, systems or practices. The demonstration project has been popular, for example, in education, agriculture, science, and elsewhere. In each case, a group of interested people has banded together to study an ideal model of an activity created by others, frequently experts. It is studied in the sense that a textbook is studied and then discussed until observers comprehend it fully. Each observer can then discover what his or her opportunities are to shift current practices to bring them in line with the practices built into the demonstration. One of the clarion calls behind the resurgence of Chinese agriculture was spoken by Mao Tse-tung under the banner "Learn from Tachai." Tachai is an agricultural commune in which barren, mountainous terrain was leveled and brought into highly productive agricultural use. Thousands upon thousands of Chinese commune workers visit Tachai year after year to study how it was done and to be inspired in the process to exploit the technology of Tachai to improve their own practices.

The idea of the demonstration project is allied to the concept of "models." The notion of a model is that some individual, group, or organization conducts itself in certain ways regarded by most to be ideal. Hence others are stimulated and encouraged to study these models and to emulate them.

Demonstration projects may be highly pertinent to everyday practices. These projects introduce a person to novel features that have not been previously experienced.

If an individual engages in activities similar to those in a demonstration project, it is possible to apply critique at a later point in time. However, this is not possible during the demonstration project itself.

Both academic learning and demonstration projects are invaluable in furthering understanding. However, critique starts at a different point than either of these methods. It is the single most powerful way of learning to strengthen future performance.

Critique initiates its approach by examining the values of and reasons for an existing practice, experience, activity, or way of doing something. That constitutes the subject matter from which learning is expected to occur. Critique, then, is a methodology of learning. It has no subject matter of its own beyond the concepts and procedures involved in using it.

What Is Critique?

Whenever two people interact in pursuit of some objective, each experiences an effort that is shared. This means that each of the participants has a reaction to what the other contributed or did not contribute to the overall achievement. If either of these individuals steps away from the effort for long enough to inspect and evaluate what in fact happened, that person is engaged in critique. This is a form of solo critique. While the event that is examined may involve another's contribution as well as one's own, the effort is basically an independent critique. If both persons were to undertake such a critique on their own, the result would simply be two solo critiques.

Critique at its best is a joint activity when two or more participants commit themselves to sharing observations to trace, based on fact, what occurred so that they can evaluate the activity and consider how it might have been done differently and better. This is an example of a shared critique of an overall experience. The purpose is to learn, in the sense of being explicit and clear, how and why the event occurred, as well as to project how the same or a similar activity might be carried out more effectively.

Critique, in other words, involves a systematic effort to examine the underlying reasons for the degree of success realized in completing an activity. It also entails describing how that activity might have been done differently to make it better. The focus, then, is always upon learning from an activity to achieve better performance in the future.

Critique is a constructive and forward-looking methodology because it centers on learning from an experience. If the activity has been done well, critique permits replication of the factors that yielded success. When an activity is carried out less than well, the new knowledge gained from critique can reduce errors in future applications.

Since both review an experience as a means of evaluating it, critique is frequently confused with criticism. Some of the content discussed in critique is the same as the content discussed during criticism. The similarity stops there because the motivtion of critique is constructive. On the other hand, criticism is more often motivated by the need of one person or group to accuse, control, or destroy another who is seen as a barrier to progress, or even as an enemy to the desired outcome.

When motivations are constructive, critique can be carried out in a way that does not create defensiveness. When criticism in the guise of critique occurs, it becomes accusing, threatening, and promotes defensiveness.

Much learning can result from critique; little from criticism.

When and How Critique Takes Place

There are three different varieties of critique. One is postmortem critique, a second is in-process critique, and a third is anticipatory critique. Within each there are several different types.

Postmortem Critique

A typical application of the idea of critique is equivalent to a "postmortem," implying that you only engage in studying an event after it is completed. Postmortem literally means "after death." It is obviously an important way of learning because, when an activity has been completed, whatever aspects of it are subject to improvement are contained within the finished activity. Thus it is a "whole," and by studying the whole it becomes possible to comprehend the principles that were involved in causing it to happen as it did.

The everyday idea of critique of the postmortem variety is captured in the idea of the "Monday-morning quarterback." The notion is that the quarterback supplies the intelligence behind a game's performance in the sense that he calls the plays, and he, therefore, makes the mistakes or exercises the wisdom, depending upon the outcome. The Monday-morning quarterback is the person who explains, after the event, what was done incorrectly and what was done well and what should have been changed to promote a better result than was achieved, or what should be repeated to ensure equally as good or better results in the future.

The "Monday-morning aspect" is of particular importance from the standpoint of understanding critique. The significance of this is that while critique undertaken that way may contribute to future performance, no amount of critique can change it.

An illustration of the postmortem approach is provided below where we hear Stan, a newly appointed president of a subsidiary company in a large international corporation, exploring with those who report to him why the "production and efficiency" (P & E) drive that was conducted last year bombed. By way of background, the situation is one where Stan's predecessor was a weak person who needed the acceptance of his subordinates and who therefore avoided any interventions with them that might create "pressure." As a result, the P & E drive was commenced, and the following is the evaluation of those who were responsible for conducting it.

Art: We sure didn't learn anything about last year's P & E drive at my meeting.

Stan: I think we did, Art. At least we got a good clue about what went on last year.

Tony: Your people don't get along with each other.

Stan: Would you call it a problem in teamwork and cooperation?

Louise: We ought to put some of these findings on the board.

Stan: That's the way we get our volunteers, Louise. Why don't you? Use the tear sheets on the easel.

Louise: Volunteered? (She get up; writes: "Problem in teamwork and cooperation")

Stan: Who's next?

Herbert: At our meeting, we remembered that after the word came down to have a P & E drive, I announced it with fanfare and hoopla to get everybody's attention. Then after the ceremonies, they say I forgot the drive itself. No followthrough. None of us paid attention to it after that.

Louise: (at easel) What'll I put down?

Robert: How about: "Announced drive and forgot it. No followthrough." That right, Bert?

Herbert: That's what they said. I'm not committing myself one way or the other.

Doris: (as Louise starts to write) Can I make a suggestion? Instead of writing down all the bad things we did, why don't we turn them around into positive pointers—for this year?

Louise: You mean like this? (Turns sheet over, writes: 1. Promote teamwork and cooperation.)

Doris: Yes. And then Bert's summary would be; let's see . . .

Herbert: How about: "Make improved productivity a way of life with followthrough." (Louise writes it down as number 2.)

Stan: We're moving now.

Tony: We never got the drive off the ground. When Phil

called for results, I asked my people what they had done. To cover up for nothing, they gave me a bunch of trumped-up stuff and I gave it to him. That was your predecessor, Stan. He bought fluff and let it go as productivity rather than seeing that we weren't really doing anything.

Stan: Okay. "Lip service rather than shared agreement on the operational meaning of being more productive."

Louise: (drawls) Tony, how would you say your point in a positive way?

Tony: "Avoid lip service substitutes."

Herbert: I'd say: "Know what real productivity is and accept no substitutes." (Louise writes this down as number 3.)[10]

Seven more reasons for the failure of the P & E drive were identified and discussed before this postmortem was completed. Needless to say, the analysis and the involvement that it produced was a critical circumstance in causing this group to shift from the idea of a "P & E" drive to a constant positive orientation to production and efficiency which eventually became a "way of life."

This is true postmortem. The experience was there to be utilized, but until Stan marshalled the group to shift their practices toward achieving improved productivity and efficiency in the future, no use was being made of the available knowledge. When Stan organized discussions to exploit a past experience from the standpoint of learning from it, it became possible to see many of the blunders and many of the reasons why the effort had not been successful and then to plan to avoid these limitations in the future.

In-Process Critique

In-process critique may also be referred to as concurrent critique. This is when critique is applied periodically from the beginning of an activity to the attainment of the goal by interrupting the work activity to study what is happening here-and-now. The idea is to change the steps that are barriers to goal attainment and to replace them with alternative procedures that would support a successful completion. The following is such an example.

There is a group consisting of several, but the interaction is between Phil, Jim, and Jeff. The group had agreed at a prior time that it would be better to critique events as they occurred rather than to wait until the end, as was the accustomed way of doing it. The underlying rationale was that by stopping and testing occurrences in the here-and-now, improvements could be introduced on the spot.

Jeff to Jim: "It looks to me as though we are going around in circles. Jim, it doesn't sound to me like you're really hearing what Phil is trying to say. It sounds more like you're chomping at the bit for him to get through so that you can repeat the same point, and you've done that several times now."

Jim to Jeff: "I think you're right. I've gotten so committed to my own point of view that I've been trying to hammer Phil down rather than trying to understand why he keeps resisting."

Jim to Phil: "Phil, have you felt that I've been hammering you down?"

Phil to Jim: "You hit the nail on the head. I don't feel like you've heard a word I've said in the last several minutes."

Jeff to Jim: "Jim, would you repeat what you think that Phil has been saying, once he has restated his position, and see if Phil will buy the notion that you understand the position that he has been advocating?"

In this in-process critique Jim had been talking past Phil. Without Jeff's intervention to examine what was really going on, two things were likely to occur. One is that Phil would eventually withdraw, with a feeling of defeat. Another is that Jim, with self-righteousness, would feel that his point of view had prevailed over other points of view that were not forcefully expressed. Phil would likely harbor a deep resentment at being ridden over roughshod by Jim. However, through in-process critique the blockage to understanding was quickly identified. We can anticipate that Jim and Phil came to an understanding of one another that resulted in an improvement in the quality of the ultimate decisions reached.

Anticipatory Critique

Anticipatory critique occurs when a deliberate effort is made to set up a model for how the activity should take place and to program actions that are consistent with the model. When this use of anticipatory critique is coupled with in-process critique, it is possible to ensure not only that the model is being applied in the way intended, but also that the model can be changed if in some way it becomes inappropriate in the light of events.

Here is a typical example of anticipatory critique.

Shipbuilders routinely provide a warranty detailing the operating specifications built into a ship and the performance standards that the owner has a right to expect in sailing that ship. This is true for passenger ships, but it is also true for tankers, freighters, and even most pleasure craft.

The conventional practice for accepting a ship from its builder is for the captain to be designated and for a crew to be drawn together. Before launching, the crew takes several days to become familiar with the ship's machinery and operating characteristics. This learning can be gained only through firsthand examination of the ship's construction and by a study of its probable performance capabilities.

The ship is then taken on a shakedown cruise, and as many defects are worked out as possible. The fact that a warranty specifies what the owner has a right to expect in terms of performance standards is forgotten, except when there is a gross malfunction. Gross malfunctions and significant departures from the warranty are reported to the captain. Many small limitations in the ship are taken for granted, with the crew working around them as best it can.

Using critique methods under these conditions, the captain would be appointed and the crew drawn together, as in the conventional case. However, before the ship is boarded, a period of time would be devoted to having the crew, as a team, learn in detail what specifications for ship performance, for machinery, and for other subcomponents are written into the warranty. Then operating manuals that specify the proper operational approach to various pieces of equipment would be consulted and critiqued for standard and unique features. Only at this point would the crew go aboard to learn about the actual properties of the ship and its equipment. During the shakedown, the ship and its equipment would be tested to their maximum and minimum limits, rather than restricting their performance to an average range. The third step is taking the ship to sea.

Sometimes critique is relied upon to discover what occurred to prevent it from occurring again, but the facts and data that have to be marshaled for the study have no human content. They are facts based upon the breakdown of machinery or equipment or a power breakdown, or any number of mechanical things; but people are not a significant component in the performance.

The Role of Feedback in Critique

The primary use of critique from the standpoint of 9,9 versatility is where the human factor is the critical ingredient and equipment and physical factors reflect human decisions rather than problems independent of them.

When these conditions prevail, the primary means of data gathering relies upon the direct experience of the participants themselves. This means that the critique is likely to be successful only when those who are participating can feed back their observations, experiences, and feelings to one another in an open, problem-solving way.

Feedback that is motivated by or is seen as criticism, promotes defensiveness. In turn, that can generate counterattack, leading those who started out to be helpful to one another into mutual recrimination, antipathy, and so on. This means that it is essential for those who are involved in a critique to be committed to carrying it out in a constructive way.

There are certain mechanical "rules" that can maximize the benefits from critique.

Feedback is received most appreciatively when it is descriptive, nonevaluative, and nonjudgmental

Nonevaluative feedback is descriptive. It pictures, in an accurate and reconstructable way, what happened in the situation and what consequences occurred as a result of what did happen. This feedback is most valuable and is less likely to generate defensiveness and counterattack, less likely to hurt and/or to cause subjective feelings of rejection. It is also less likely to be seen as a threat of expulsion, or as a communication that suggests that a person is losing popularity.

The closer the feedback is to the event it describes, the better it is

When an event and the critique of it occur in close connection with one another, it is easier for the person whose behavior is being described to reconstruct the actual event and the thoughts, feelings, and emotions surrounding it. This greater capacity for reconstruction enables the person to learn more fully because he or she can "identify" with it and so understand his or her role in it.

Small units of feedback, but not trivia, should be offered

A person can be offered feedback that is specific, concrete, and limited enough in magnitude to enable it to be thoroughly understood. This is better than a general assessment that is so lacking in specific detail that it is difficult to understand fully what it is attempting to convey.

On the other hand, trivia, or things of little or no importance, have little bearing on the important aspects of personal effectiveness and so contribute very little to personal learning.

Concentrate on things a person can change

Those things a person has a reasonable prospect of doing something about are far more worthy topics of feedback than are things a person is highly unlikely to be able to change. Since feedback is expected to form a basis for change, the more it relates to things that can be changed, the more useful the feedback will be. It might be more comfortable to concentrate on characteristics and conditions not in need of change, but this is not desirable in the context of learning to be more effective.

Be aware of the personal motivations for giving feedback

An individual is most helpful to others when he or she is aware of the underlying motivations that stimulate the urge to give feedback. This motivation is often a 9,9 orientation of concern for contributing to others through a caring attitude toward them. However, feedback opportunities can be used, for example, to score a point or to reap vengeance, and this characterizes what might be the extreme motivation of a 9,1-oriented person. By comparison, a 1,9-oriented person might give positive feedback to be endeared to the recipient. A 1,1-oriented person might do so to show that he or she is "with it," even though the underlying attitude is "I couldn't care less." A 5,5-oriented person is motivated to offer feedback to communicate that the recipient is a valued person, and in this way an increment of popularity is gained by the person who gives it.

In comparison with these, the 9,9-oriented person, motivated by the desire to make a contribution through caring for the effectiveness of others, is most likely to offer feedback intended to bring about heightened performance and thereby improve feelings of self-worth.

When Is Critique Useful?

Critique may be used when

- Work is bogged down and people are unclear as to the causes of their lack of progress.

- Work practices have been relatively formal and there is a readiness to move toward informality and more spontaneous collaboration
- A new procedure is being introduced.
- A group is embarking on an innovative activity, such as making a new policy, understanding a new issue or concept, designing a new service and so forth.
- A group's membership is changed, particularly by the introduction of a new boss.
- 9,9 teamwork values are understood by team members who are motivated to learn how to increase their effectiveness.

Critique is not likely to be useful when

- Two or more participants are overtly antagonistic to one another and would use the opportunity for criticism.
- There is a crisis and the time needed for deliberation is unavailable.
- Activities are relatively mechanical and of such a routine nature that few benefits can be ancitipated by submitting them to examination and study.
- Participants are inexperienced in face-to-face feedback methods or fearful of open communication.

SUMMARY

Critique is the most powerful means available for learning from experience. When other principles of behavior are understood and efforts are being made to manage according to them, then it becomes feasible to introduce critique as one important way of strengthening performance.

There are three different orientations to critique. One is anticipatory critique, i.e., studying and projecting the particular activities that will be involved in a program before the program is launched to avoid the errors and mistakes that come from moving into an activity with minimum planning and with reliance on intuition, impulse, or common sense. A second kind of critique is in-process critique, which involves interrupting an activity to study the under-lying assumptions that people are making, the attitudes that people are expressing, and the actions that they are engaged in that may or may not be productive of solid teamwork. A third approach is to critique after the fact, postmortem. This entails studying a completed activity, not to change it but, rather, to take advantage of whatever is learned for the improvement of future work.

Because critique and criticism are basically close to one another, it becomes important that individuals, groups, and teams engaging in critique keep these two separate, avoiding criticism and exploiting critique. When what was intended to be critique becomes criticism, it only enlarges the arena of controversy rather than promoting the devel-opment of shared understanding and insight. For this reason rules of feedback that can facilitate the sound utilization of critique have been provided to promote conditions condu-cive to generating increased effectiveness.

11
Norms and Standards

One of the great (or greatest) mysteries of modern management is concerned with why a number of concepts that have proved very powerful for strengthening managerial effectiveness have been given so little attention. These concepts are not difficult to understand. They make sense and are easy to apply. Only through their use can we even hope to approach the solution to many chronic problems today's managers face.

**The Concepts
Themselves**

These concepts relate to the role of norms and standards in regulating behavior. When norms and standards exercise a controlling effect on behavior, it is important to know what these norms and standards are and how to manage or change them to what they should be, as a basis for promoting productivity and organization excellence.

The following may help you understand some of the reasons why insufficient attention has been paid to norms and standards.

As we study our own day-by-day experiences, we see ourselves as exercising informed free choice independently of what others may be doing. If others agree with us, well and good. If they do not, we often explain differences in personal behavior by saying they are related to the concept of individuality. Each of us thinks in unique and distinctive ways and is motivated in distinctive ways. Therefore, there is no reason we should be expected to come to the same conclusions, except when they are very obvious. Furthermore, as we observe others, we see they are not exactly like us and we center on their uniqueness and distinctiveness. This pursuit of individuality has received much support in the last several decades.

When we observe ourselves or when we observe our colleagues, what we are likely to "miss" is the degree to which all of us conform to similar and sometimes almost identical patterns of behavior. In the small groups in which people interact, we find similar attitudes toward the organization, its products or services, how good it is as a place in which to be employed, what constitutes a fair day's work, and a host of other attitudes that are shared. We know, however, that they are not shared by everyone in the organization. The second aspect of norms that we fail to see is that the norms to which we commit ourselves are related to what others, especially those with whom we interact and identify, think. If the "others" whom we are observing are not in our primary group, then the view that "everybody thinks differently" receives increasing confirmation, depending on the degree of difference between us and them. It is only when we examine the extent to which personal attitudes, thoughts, and feelings are shared with other members of our primary group that the regulating effect of informal norms and standards becomes clearly visible.

Another aspect of norms and standards is that their regulating effect is present but hidden, particularly when norms are informal. This means that the norms that regulate our behavior have not been deliberately worked out or made explicit as topics of discussion and agreement. The norms themselves have not been identified. They exist and influence us, but we are largely unfamiliar with them.

When norms become rules and regulations, they become clear to us. If we agree with these norms, we automatically expect everyone to comply with them. Some norms have become rules and regulations of a kind with which we are all familiar—driving on the correct side of the road, resisting the temptation to make U-turns, obeying traffic signals, and a number of others that relate to transportation. A moment's reflection tells us that when people conform to rules such as these, everyone's freedom to move is increased; when they are violated, the situation becomes chaotic and personal safety is endangered.

On the other hand, when norms that are seen as constraining are imposed on us, or when we disagree with existing rules and regulations, our underlying thoughts are often focused on ways to violate them, although an appearance of conformity may be maintained. Rather than embracing the established norms, we reject them, and if we cannot disobey them, we constantly complain about their restrictive and arbitrary quality.

There is a deeper significance in these everyday examples. It is that managers and workers alike, within their own primary membership groups, share an endless number of norms and standards in terms of which lateral influence is exercised by one person on another to think and act in the same way. For the most part managers completely disregard the existence of norms and standards. They are unaware of how to manage them or how to change them. Therefore, situations tend to degenerate into circumstances where the least common denominator system of norms prevails. What is needed to bring norms and standards under sound management is the conceptual understanding and managerial skill to (1) identify organizational norms and standards, (2) recognize when they are adverse to high productivity and satisfaction with work, and (3) design and execute the changes necessary for shifting from one set of norms and standards to another that is more supportive of productivity and more rewarding in terms of satisfaction.

An Organization's Norms and Standards

While there is an endless variety of norms and standards in an organization, the following descriptions identify those with which the reader is likely to be familiar and to understand in terms of past experience or observation.

On first examination, it might be thought that having an accident is a highly individual affair. Some people are accident prone, while others are not. To a degree this is an accurate statement, but it misses the deeper point of how norms and standards influence safety.

We also know that different organizations in which people are doing the same kind of work differ widely with respect to the frequency with which accidents occur. In Situation A, the accident rate is low. In Situation B, it is high. This may be due to selection: Those working in Situation A may have been selected for their carefulness, while those in Situation B were selected for some other reason. Alternatively, the explanation for the difference may be that the informal norms that people share about taking physical risks, being responsible for one another, and so on, are different in the two situations.

What are the norms and standards of those who work in primary group settings where the accident rate is low although the probability of having accidents is high? One is a commonsense concern for working according to safe practices. Another is that each person feels responsible for ensuring that co-workers are working safely. When these two norms are widely shared, the frequency of accidents is significantly reduced. On the other hand, when management applies pressure in the pursuit of greater productivity, people may be inclined to violate the norms and standards of safe working practices. When this happens, the accident rate will increase.

Numerous demonstrations are available for showing how accidents, conceived as an end result of norms and standards, can be brought under managerial control. The strategy for doing so is first to enable individuals who work under conditions likely to produce accidents to diagnose why accidents occur. Next, through open discussion, these individuals can identify the norms of safe practice that they are prepared to adhere to and to which they will be committed. When this has been done, the rate of accident frequency is diminished. Productivity is more likely to be increased, rather than reduced, when people take responsibility for their own safety. This happens for many reasons, ranging from growing pride in good output made safely to the simple truth that fewer accidents mean less lost time.

Other comparable examples of shifting behavior that is controlled by norms and standards involve reducing the amount of waste, changing the product quality level, reducing the frequency of absences, reducing late starts, eliminating early quitting, and so on.

At higher levels of management, the controlling effects of norms and standards are quite evident, too. When executives share the informal norm that "X is about the best rate of improvement that we can expect," then they are "locked in" to that rate of growth. No one is able to challenge it and the creative thinking needed for seeing how to advance the rate simply has no opportunity to blossom. Another example is the norm concerned with "shared loyalty to a product line." Under these circumstances, product innovation or diversification is unlikely to have any realistic opportunity to occur.

The Theory of and Research into the Regulating Effects of Shared Norms and Standards

One of the most thoroughly researched and documented studies in the behavioral field concerns the power a group exercises over its individual members. The earliest demonstrations were in the thirties when college students, as guinea pigs, were asked to make judgments about the rate of movement of a light occurring in a visual field.[11] The problem involved the "autokinetic" effect. This is the effect that anyone can experience on a dark, clear night when looking at a star. The star is seen to move, sometimes erratically, sometimes swiftly. In fact, the movement does not really occur.

The effect can be created under laboratory conditions in the following way. A person in a darkened room is asked to look toward the back of the room (not knowing how far he or she is from the back wall) where a pinpoint of light is visible. Soon the light will begin to move, and the observer is asked to report on the number of inches or feet that the light traverses in a specific period of time.

To this situation we now add a "confederate." The confederate is "programmed," or instructed in advance of each trial period to report how much movement he or she observed just before the experimental subject reports. We can then study how the first person's report of movement affects the uninformed subject. The conclusion is that the uninformed subject, though he or she has no way of knowing or even recognizing it, is influenced significantly by the confederate's answers.

A reaction the reader might have to this experiment is, "Well, that is in the character of the autokinetic effect, but it tells little about how primary groups influence the attitudes and behavior of their members."

The next series of experiments changed the demonstration problem. Experimental subjects were asked to compare the length of two lines, where determining which was longer and which was shorter was a relatively simple task. Another change involved adding additional "subjects" (also programmed) who gave incorrect reports as to which of the two lines was shorter or longer just before the experimental subject reported. It was then possible to study how much influence was exerted on one individual by another by noting the number of legitimate subjects who were prepared to say—after hearing the incorrect report of the "programmed" subjects—that the longer line was shorter than the obviously shorter line.[12]

In this experiment, the social effect of reports by another person was least when there was only one other person. When two others were present, the social effect became strong, and approximately one-third of all "guinea pig subjects" reported inaccurately. Furthermore, a significant percent of these subjects whose reports were in error never became aware of the discrepancy between the visual evidence they could directly observe and the inaccurate response they gave.

The experiments took a different turn when the guinea pig subject received support from one of the confederates. During the reporting trials, one of the confederates would shift from giving uniformly inaccurate responses to giving accurate responses. The experimental subject was then somewhat freed from the group pressure previously experienced and was able to report an accurate reaction. This shows the extent to which just one ally in a group situation can help a person maintain independence and freedom from social pressures.

In all of these experiments there is always a minority of individuals who are independent and able to maintain objective judgment, even in the face of pressures from other members in the situation. However, group pressure tends to exert a very strong influence on most people. This important finding partly explains the brainwashing that took place in Korea. One of the "tricks" of brainwashing was to separate the natural leaders in the prisoner groups from the rest. Without natural leaders capable of maintaining independence from brainwashing, the rest of the prisioners succumbed to the efforts of their captors.

There are other aspects of this basic demonstration of the pervasive nature of social pressures, but the above are sufficient to let us identify the problem. If the exercise of power and authority is seen as vertical influence, i.e., influence that cascades from one level down to another, then the capacity of one's immediate associates unintentionally to exercise controlling influences on one another can be viewed as lateral power.

Among the earliest industrial demonstrations of the influence of informal norms and standards on productivity are studies of individuals at both ends of the conformity continuum. Every productivity group has its own norm by which its members abide. However, "rate-busters" are people who work beyond the informal norm that regulates others. In doing so, rate-busters make the others look bad by comparison. There is a strong tendency for those who are embarrassed by the rate-buster to take corrective action. One way of doing so is to isolate the rate-buster and in this way to withdraw any social support that he or she might otherwise have enjoyed.

At the opposite end of the conformity continuum is the "goldbrick." Goldbricks are people who do not pull their share of the load. The amount that a person should contribute is informally agreed to within the work group. Again, the goldbrick is subject to ostracism, but this time for not making the required contribution. Both rate-buster and goldbrick demonstrate the meaning of "breaking ranks." There are few co-workers who are more subject to the dislike and antagonisms of their workmates than those who in these ways do not "stick together," observing the standards of the majority.

The widespread existence of norms and standards, then, can be accepted as fact. Many are seen not to be subject to control, and it then appears there is no way to change them. This is true even when those who are influenced by the existing norms and standards would really prefer to be able to operate according to more progressive ones. Not knowing how to change them, people quickly come to "play the game" because in those circumstances being esteemed by one's work colleagues is far more important than being productive and provoking the wrath of one's co-workers.

The conditions essential for bringing into being and maintaining valid norms and standards that support productivity involve sound managerial use of the principles of behavior introduced in chapter 2. When these are violated, the norms and standards by which people work are unlikely to be consistent with goals of high productivity, good quality of output, good profit, or an economic return on the investment of money and effort.

Of greatest importance for creating a climate favorable to changing norms is the exercise of power and authority in a 9,9 manner. When this occurs, involvement is high, and active participation in thinking about problems includes the members of all primary groups. Under these conditions, members can openly discuss how they feel about the norms and standards by which they operate without feeling guilty for revealing secrets or "helping" management. Rather, the basic attitude is the reverse. Helping management to be more productive becomes accepted as a part of everyone's responsibility.

Norms in Union-Management Relations

A final example may be useful for showing the pervasive influences of norms and standards. It involves a win-lose struggle between a militant union and a reactionary company. The union had slowly but surely committed itself to a norm that said, "We will teach management a lesson it will never forget." The management attitude over this same period had become, "The union is evil. It is led by self-serving union officers who are being manipulated by the national body. The reason they respond to this manipulation is that they look forward to moving into the union headquarters."

These two sets of conflicting norms prevailed to such a degree that a union leader who "listened" to management was a "traitor to the cause" by violating the shared norms of the members of the union. A manager who could insult a union officer and get away with it was a "hero" for successfully dealing another blow to the enemy. Under these conditions, sharp win-lose antagonisms inevitably led to the kind of confrontation where fixed positions prevailed. The overriding goal was to defeat the "enemy." [13]

Eventually, the key executive in management came to see the dead-end quality of this power struggle and became convinced that the long-term health of the company and its employees could only be served by creating a problem-solving relationship with the union.

But how? If the manager announced this goal as an edict, it would be resisted, resented, and defeated. Furthermore, he would be seen as a poor leader seeking to curry favor for a short-term gain that would serve only to build even greater strength into the already destructive union leadership. Therefore, he and the executive leadership agreed to explore among themselves in an open discussion the attitudes they shared toward the union and where these attitudes had come from, and to answer the question, "Does there exist any possibility of rectifying this bad situation?" The management team did this, and after an intensive discussion of several hours came to the conclusion that the only "future" for the company lay in bringing about a better relationship with the union. They further agreed that the only realistic way of attempting to do so would be to "treat the union officers with dignity and respect by virtue of their being elected representatives of their members."

Of course, the fact that a group of twelve or thirteen top executives shifted their norms of behavior did not trigger the immediate shift in behavior of the hundreds of other managers who had long been guided by norms of animosity and had learned to excel in the ability to provoke the union. Thus, it became necessary for all managers, down to front-line foremen, to come together and answer the same questions as those dealt with by the top management team. After a period of time, an organization-wide norm emerged: "treating the union officers with dignity and respect. . . ."

Once this norm became shared, it was still not easy to apply. Persistence and steadfastness were still needed to aid managers to learn the extent to which their behavior had been disrespectful and destructive. As these managers began to exercise constraint upon themselves, the union leaders noticed the difference but were unsure of how to react. They had learned how to do battle with an adversary, but now they had no adversary.

The management was not saying "yes" to union demands, but it was not saying "no" either. Every real problem that was brought to the bargaining table was treated as a real problem to which better and poorer solutions existed. The persistence of management in maintaining these open discussions until the deeper underlying problems of animosity could be reduced and the real problem identified, slowly but surely brought to light the changes essential for solving the problems. Once the union began to see the emergence of feasible solutions, in the place of what previously had been total frustration at not even being able to get a realistic hearing, enthusiasm for solving problems increased and a mutual trust and respect began to develop. Collaboration with the union expanded to involve the discussion of many problems that had become chronic but had lain dormant over an extended period of time.

This story has many implications, but primarily it serves as a useful description of (1) the norms and standards that control the behavior of all individuals who share membership, (2) the pervasiveness of the norms for regulating behavior and ensuring the maintenance of antagonisms, (3) the managerial strategy for gaining a shift in norms and standards among its entire membership, and (4) the resultant behavior that dramatically shifted the union-management relationship. All of these factors support the conclusion initially reached in the introduction.

SUMMARY

In conclusion, it seems that norms and standards are ignored by modern management, and yet the research and organizational demonstrations of how to change them have shown this area of management to be one of the easiest to change. This is so because the concepts are clear and easily understood. Once a sound understanding of them has been gained, the strategies and tactics for changing actual problems of productivity are within our reach.

12
Solving Problems in a 9,9-Oriented Way

$\mathbf{A}$ problem occurs whenever an existing condition prevents some desired outcome from happening or when a discrepancy is exposed between what "is" and what "should be." Problem solving is different from a creative effort, in that creativity is the process involving the discovery of something previously not known, i.e., identifying what should be.

Many managers have been exposed to the classic problem-solving model, which includes a multistep sequence: First, define the problem; second, develop alternative solutions to it; third, evaluate the alternatives; fourth, select the most desirable alternative; fifth, implement.[14] There are variations in how each of these steps is done, but they are relatively unimportant. This rational description of problem solving is useful as a mechanical sequence, but because it disregards the human side, it can be severely limiting in its usefulness.

The Human Side of Problem-Solving

The resulting approach is far different from that described above because additional considerations come into focus, which must be dealt with soundly if the best solution is to be found.

Felt Problem or Real Problem

One of these considerations is being sure that the felt

problem is the real problem. Frequently the problem that managers feel a need to solve is not the real problem at all, and there is no assurance that solving the felt problem will make any contribution to solving the real problem.

When the Felt Problem Is Not the Real Problem. An example of a felt problem expressed in many companies is communication difficulty. The attitude is "If we could only solve our communication problems, many of our other difficulties would clear up." As a result, company after company has gone into media programs of various sorts: company papers, video cassette presentations, programs for aiding managers to acquire better platform skills, gripe sessions, seminars on listening, and so on. Yet they find that no matter how much effort is put into solving communication difficulties, problems continue to exist. Difficulty of communication was merely a symptom.

What Is the Real Problem? The problem that explains the communications problem is far more likely to be the misuse of power and authority throughout the hierarchy. Trying to solve the real problem with a media blitz contributes little or nothing to its ultimate resolution.

Take another example. A company with a sizable real-estate holding built various production units in one corner of the available space. This was done for reasons of economy. Therefore, it was simpler and less expensive to build a new unit onto an existing one and take advantage of utilities already provided. The felt problem in this case was conserving utilities. This was done successfully.

But the wrong problem had been solved. The symptoms had been treated, rather than the cause. The add-on produced such chronic congestion that the company was limited in expansion possibilities. The real problem, which had not been recognized, was how to provide for orderly expansion according to a basic plan and yet be in a position to take advantage of emerging opportunities. Providing a blueprint of the infrastructure for the longterm would have solved the "problem."

The solution of felt problems as contrasted with real ones requires less diagnosis, less planning, and less short-term risk. If the real problem remains unsolved, however, chronic or adverse side effects are likely to appear. Eventually the organization or its responsible individuals are "forced" to either abandon effort or to grapple with the real problem, usually after much unnecessary frustration and expense.

Identifying the real problem in the beginning is an invaluable managerial skill. On the physical side, this means effective utilization of various engineering and financial disciplines. On the human side the demand is for effective behavioral and organizational diagnosis.

When managers acquire skills of effective behavioral and organization diagnosis, they no longer will continue to solve problems that are immediately felt but will turn their attention to the real problems.

Whose Problem Is It?

A second important attribute in defining the problem is the ability to identify those individuals who have the know-how and responsibility essential for successfully grappling with it. The "Whose Problem Is It?" question is anything but simple, even though on the surface it may appear straightforward. If the "wrong" people solve the problem, it is less likely to stay solved than if the "right" people are involved in finding a solution to it.

The issue of "Whose Problem Is It?" is dealt with elsewhere in this book. Only a brief reconstruction of the strategy needs to be reintroduced at this time.

The problem may belong to one person and this person may be the boss or a subordinate team member. In any event, that person working alone has the capacity and resources essential for solving the problem. Others can contribute nothing more to the solution, and drawing them in is a waste. The same basic logic applies to other groupings. The problem may involve only two members, a boss and a subordinate, or two colleagues. It may involve several, it may involve all team members; in some cases, additional people from outside the team may have the know-how essential for dealing with the issue at hand.

Criteria for "Whose Problem Is It?" are available in the table on page 83. This table may be consulted and utilized in answering the question as to who should be involved in solving the real problem.

Identifying both the real problem and those who should be involved in finding a solution to it, then, are the important first two steps.

Developing Criteria of a Sound Solution

Before developing or identifying alternatives for solving a problem, it is important that criteria against which to evaluate the various solutions be developed to measure soundness and identify adverse side effects. This step is frequently omitted. The result is that when alternatives are formulated, vested interests come into play that increase the difficulty of choosing the soundest alternative. Again, the human side intrudes as a barrier to the exercise of sound business logic.

Developing the criteria for a sound solution encourages participants to focus on the character of the solution itself rather than on the extent to which the solution might be favorable or unfavorable from personal perspectives. Having reached agreement on criteria, participants are then committed to utilizing these criteria in evaluating various alternatives rather than trying to promote a solution most favorable to themselves.

Developing Alternatives

The classic or rational approach encourages managers to identify the full range of options available as opposed to implementing the first "reasonable" possibility that presents itself. Basic and sound examination of the full range of options, before deciding on a particular course of action, allows possibilities to be seen that might otherwise never come under consideration. For this reason the best solution is more likely to emerge.

Selecting the Best Available Solution

With explicit criteria for evaluating a sound solution

and the right people engaged in searching for the solution, and with all available options and alternatives examined, the real test is whether or not the soundest approach actually can be agreed upon and implemented.

Those responsible for solving the problem are still likely to disagree on the best solution. Some of this disagreement may arise from hidden agenda, vested interests, and—sometimes—simply from an insufficient background in "feeling" the most probable consequences of each alternative. The 9,9 way of dealing with this problem is to confront differences and air reservations and doubts openly. When differences can be resolved in the open, members are more able to agree on the best solution and to give commitment to its effective implementation.

Designing the Implementation

Many difficulties are encountered in implementation, though the classic model makes little or no provision for eliminating them. These also need to be resolved as part and parcel of a problem-solving cycle.

One of the major problems with implementation involves time pressures from other ongoing activities. While those responsible for implementation may have the capability, the commitment, and so on, other problems may arise that command their attention. Attention is drawn away from the implementation toward grappling with ongoing problems and the implementation "dies." By anticipating time pressures from other demands that may be of higher priority than efforts to solve the problem, it becomes possible simultaneously to search for ways of dealing with other problems and to implement the solution of the earlier problem. Another barrier to effective implementation arises when resources necessary for solving the problem may not be available because their existence was presumed and no effort was made to ensure that they would be provided. When this aspect of implementation is anticipated, it becomes possible to test for availability of resources and to avoid the frustration that comes from commitment to an action that is impossible to carry out. Contingencies can be introduced for dealing with unanticipated needs for resources should they arise.

Critique

Once the solution is implemented, the next step is to study why it worked. Seldom mentioned as an attribute of the classic problem-solving model, this particular kind of critique is called postmortem critique. All those who have been engaged in or concerned with the problem in any way are involved. Upon conclusion of the project they study the entire cycle to spot limitations in all phases of the problem-solving cycle. Critique of this sort is an invaluable learning aid. It ensures that mistakes made in one problem-solving cycle will be identified so that steps may be taken to avoid repeating them. Critique may be the most valuable aspect of the 9,9 versatility approach because it provides a basis for coupling problem solving with learning.

SUMMARY

The 9,9 approach to solving problems has been contrasted with the classic problem-solving model. This comparison leads to the conclusion that the classic model is not wrong, but it is significantly limited by failure to use it in the context of the human side of problem solving.

When the human side of problem solving is integrated into the classic model, numerous differences in how it is employed in a constructive way become evident. These include the recognition that the felt problem often is not the real problem and that a diagnostic strategy is preferable to a common-sense definition of the problem. Another consideration is that those involved in problem solving often are not the "right" ones. There may be too many, too few, or the wrong people involved. Some problems are best solved 1/0, some 1/1, some 1/some, and still other problems on a 1/all basis. Some may not be solved even on a 1/all basis because outsiders are essential to finding and implementing a sound solution. Trying to solve a problem without mobilizing the necessary human resources is to risk failure.

Developing criteria for an elegant solution is a desirable step because it focuses thought and attention on the properties a best solution could contain. Commitment to one solution over another comes later, after Alternative A has been compared with Alternative B, A and B with C, and so on, all in the light of criteria.

Evaluation of the alternatives appears to be a rational step, but here, too, human elements intrude in the form of vested interests, hidden agenda, and so on, to distort solution selection. This is so, even though criteria of a sound solution may previously have been developed. The 9,9 approach is to aid participants to bring forth reservations and doubts and to confront resistances directly, so that any person resisting can explore and evaluate reasons for resistance. If the resistance is real it can benefit problem solving; when unreal it can be eliminated from consideration.

The planning step for implementation often is ignored, with the result that other organization pressures act on those who are responsible for implementation, thus making it impossible to bring an effective solution into use. Furthermore, the resources essential for effective implementation may not have been anticipated in the planning stage and may be unavailable to permit implementation.

Postmortem critique of problem solving is stepping away from the entire cycle and exploring strengths and weaknesses of decisions made at each step from beginning to end. In this way the members involved gain insight as to what should be retained and repeated—or identified and eliminated—in future problem-solving cycles.

The 9,9 versatility approach leads to the use of the problem-solving model along with the effective mobilization of the human resources essential for bringing a valid solution to bear.

13
Change

The purpose of presenting behavioral science principles in such detail in this book is to enable you to test practices that prevail in your organization and, beyond that, to examine your own ways of working with and through others in light of them. You probably have seen many gaps and discrepancies between what occurs in practice in your organization's life and what could be expected if these principles were in daily use. When such gaps and discrepancies prevail, it can be accepted that productivity suffers, as do satisfaction and creativity, and the stiuation itself may have an adverse impact on physical and mental health.

The issue, then, of how to shift from current practices of management to stronger and more effective practices based on behavioral science principles is of vital significance. To speak about change is well and good. In fact, though, change is something far more difficult to accomplish than just saying, "Okay, I see it; I'll change it."

Many changes *can* be introduced in this way, but they almost always constitute small departures from current practices. In other words, the gap or discrepancy between characteristic practices of the past and the desired practices of the future is very minor.

Bringing about the kind of change necessary to implement behavioral science principles is far more complex and subtle. Therefore, in this chapter we want to deal with some considerations related to change that must be understood and dealt with if efforts to change are to be successful.

The first question is who you are relative to others in your organization; that is, "Who's in charge?" If you are in charge, your ability to effect change is far different than if you are not in charge. We want to deal with how to go about the introduction of change under both sets of conditions.

There is a straightforward answer to this question. If you are the top man, you are in charge. This means that there is no one in a position above you from whom you have to get approval or authorization or to whom you must go for consent. There may be others associated with you to whom you go for counsel or for guidance, but you shoulder the ultimate responsibility for decisions that are made.

Are You the Person in Charge?

If you are the chief executive officer of a company or the director of an agency, the likelihood is very great that you are the person in charge. As a chief executive officer you may have a board of directors, and for certain special problems it may be necessary to gain its approval. But insofar as the manner of utilizing the organization's resources is concerned, you are the person ultimately in charge. If you decide to take the steps necessary to bring sound principles of behavior into everyday use, you can do this under your own responsibilities.

The situation is not quite so clear if you are the head of a subsidiary or if you are the manager of a plant, a district, or a region. Under these conditions, you may or may not be the person in charge, even though your job description says that you are the responsible person.

The key test of whether you are the person in charge is whether you have budget approval authority for expending funds on human resource development.

If you do not have such approval authority, the likelihood is that you are not the person in charge. Even here, though, there may be exceptions.

The most important exception is this. If those above you relate with you in such a way that you tell them what you want, they review it, probe your reasoning, but uniformly give their approval, then for all practical purposes you are still the person in charge. If you are not the top person, and if you do not have approving authority, then you are not the person in charge.

Assuming that you are the person in charge, we can now deal with the question of how you can bring change about.

Nine fundamental principles of behavior that emerge from behavioral science research and theory were identified in chapter 2. You will recognize that these principles of human relationships are difficult for any individual to practice in isolation or to adhere to if they are being grossly violated by others. Therefore the issue is to change underlying principles of behavior that characterize the entire human system of organization, not just an individual or team.

This awareness has led to the concept of organization development, which means seeing the organization as the unit of change, rather than individuals on a one-by-one basis.

Three Approaches to Organization Development (OD)

There are three broadly different approaches to the introduction of change in human behavior. These have been widely written about and described. The sketches provided below, however, will convey the underlying assumptions about change on which each is based.

Technique-Centered OD

Technique-centered OD is what the name implies: attempting to bring about change by introducing a new technique. One of the best known examples of technique-centered OD is management-by-objectives. Management-by-objectives has become a mechanical system that involves collaboration between bosses and subordinates to set objectives, with the subordinates then being held accountable for achieving the agreed-upon objectives. The mechanics of technique-centered management-by-objectives are complex and the paperwork is extensive. The strategy itself is basically simple.

Other examples of technique-centered OD include job enrichment, flexi-time scheduling, and survey research, and a number of others. All of these approaches are technique-centered because they involve introducing managers to a new or different way of managing, with no preliminary thinking to enable each manager to investigate his own Grid style and to learn sound and unsound principles as the basis for using these techniques. The various techniques have been grouped together under the title "quality of work life" as an approach to strengthening organization effectiveness. Quality of work life is now coming under criticism for the reasons about to be discussed.

A 9,1-oriented manager is likely to embrace the mechanics of management-by-objectives in a whole-hearted way. This is not, however, because the manager sees it as a way of aiding subordinates to strengthen their contributions. Rather, it is a technique of managing that enables the 9,1-oriented manager to strengthen his or her mastery, domination, and control over subordinates by "forcing" subordinates to identify and agree to goals that they then commit themselves to reach.

In a comparable manner, a 1,9-oriented manager may embrace management-by-objectives and then "invite" subordinates to set their own objectives at whatever level of excellence they may be prepared to embrace. The boss does not critique or help the subordinates think through what would be important goals for them to seek to accomplish. For a 1,9-oriented manager to do so would be an excessive intrusion, at least from the manager's point of view. In fact, it might lead to disagreement, and 1,9-oriented managers feel that they are risking personal rejection when they encounter conflict with anyone. Comparable distortions of management-by-objectives are evident when a manager's basic orientation is 1,1, 5,5, or paternalistic. The point is that any technique-centered approach to change tends to be distorted in the direction of the Grid style of the person who is implementing the technique. As a result, many sound ways of strengthening managerial effectiveness are aborted by the manner in which they are brought into being. Technique-centered OD has been found to be unsatisfactory time and time again, but managers persist in repeating the mistake over and over, being unaware of the impact of Grid style on the utilization of an otherwise neutral technique.

Process-Centered OD

A second approach to increasing the effectiveness of behavior in organizations is process-centered OD. This is an approach that involves managers in studying their own behavior, and this aspect is basically sound. However, the manner in which this learning takes place causes it to be weak and, for the most part, ineffective.

The basic approach to process-centered OD is for the teams of the organization to study their own characteristic behavior to identify problems and correct them. This is done by relying on an outside expert who meets with the team to facilitate the discussion of its difficulties. This diminishes the likelihood that open hostilities will break out.

The catalyst, or facilitator, goes about this in one of two ways. One is to interview or in some other way collect data from group members to find out how they see their own group dynamics. The catalyst then summarizes the conclusions and reports back to the group in such a manner as to enable them to discuss the data. Alternatively, the catalyst may meet with the group for face-to-face discussion, aiding group members to bring forward facts and feelings about the group's dynamics.

In either of these approaches, the catalytic way of learning about group process suffers from two fatal weaknesses. One has its roots in the intermediary role played by the catalyst or facilitator. Participants have not learned how to use open communication; the catalyst provides a "crutch" that enables them to do so. The catalyst is always present and is the one who provides the assurance that everything is okay. Therefore, group members never do learn how to communicate openly.

The second fatal weakness is the same as was introduced in the context of technique-centered OD. Learning about principles of behavior has been bypassed and reliance placed on the manager's "common sense," the very source of guidance that resulted in difficulties in the first place.

Experience with process-centered OD can be interpreted in the following way. Participants find it a useful procedure and are encouraged that it will enable them to solve their problems. This is the early reaction. A later reaction is that while what was studied was relevant to increasing their effectiveness, they are unable to make significant use of what was learned in the absence of the catalyst or facilitator. This is the problem of catalyst-in versus catalyst-out. When the catalyst is in the situation, participants can use his or her model and rely upon it to increase the effectiveness of their discussion. When the catalyst is absent, they seem unable to transfer what has been learned.

Grid-Centered OD

The third approach to OD rests upon aiding all managers of an organization to learn the Grid theories in personal terms that clarify to each the current ways in which they try to achieve production with and through people, and (2) helping them learn the skills necessary for moving into a 9,9 orientation, using sound principles of behavior. This approach to OD is basic. Once it has been brought into use, the 9,9 values and ways of behaving become the norms and standards that guide the organization in what constitutes sound behavior.

Phases of Grid OD

Before describing the six stages or phases of development for bringing Grid-centered OD into organization use, it is important to consider how Grid OD gets introduced into an organization. This is a major factor in its success.

Steps for Getting into Organization-wide Grid Development

Background Reading   Gives an orientation as to how ap-

	plied behavioral science is being used to strengthen organizations
Seeding	Provides a few organization members deep insight into Phase 1 and the Grid without the organization's being committed to doing more
Grid OD Seminar	Gives a few managers a breadth and depth of insight into the whole of Grid OD as the basis for evaluation and possible recommendations for next steps
Pilot Grid Seminar	Provides the organization a test-tube trial of what would be involved were the organization to engage in Phase 1
Pilot Teamwork Development	Affords the top team direct understanding of how the Grid is applied to strengthening not only its team effectiveness, but also the effectiveness of individuals as the basis for assessing probable impact of Phase 2 applied on an organization-wide basis[15]

Finding a way to achieve an organization-wide awareness and conviction about the importance of Grid OD among all members without demanding participation is the dilemma. The best approach lies in a series of preliminary exploratory steps designed to orient members to possibilities, as suggested in the table above. These steps permit the organization to test the implications of Grid OD in a step-wise way without any obligation to become deeply involved in it. If these steps are taken in a planned way, organization members have the opportunity to develop their own commitments through a series of self-convincing experiences. Orientation without obligation—the opportunity to test the temperature before plunging in—produces awareness of possibilities from which a conviction-based decision can be made.

Grid Phase 1

In the initial phase of organization development everyone in the organization gets involved in learning the Grid and using it to evaluate personal styles of managing. This is made possible through attending a five-day seminar.

Maximum impact is possible when all employees participate. Included are persons who manage others, though some companies begin by extending organization development to include technical, wage-earning, and salaried personnel. The decision on extending Grid learning to other than managerial levels can be made at a later time.

Grid Seminar Goals

Seminar has four major goals.

1 Gain personal learning by
—understanding the Grid as a framework of thought,
—gaining insight into one's own Grid style,
—increasing personal objectivity in work behavior,
—reexamining managerial values, and
—developing a common language for communicating about behavior.

2 Experience problem solving in teams by
—testing ways to increase effectiveness,
—studying the use of critique,
—developing standards for openness and candor, and
—examining the need for active listening.

3 Learn about managing intergroup conflict by
—studying barriers between teams,
—examining conflict within teams, and
—exploring ways of reducing or eliminating such conflicts.

4 Comprehend organization implications by

—understanding impact of work culture on behavior and

—gaining appreciation of Grid OD and possible outcomes.

These seminars involve hard work. The program requires thirty or more hours of guided study before the seminar week itself, which usually begins Sunday evening and runs through the following Friday. Participants are involved in learning activities morning, afternoon, and evening.

The sessions include investigation by each person of managerial approaches and alternate ways of managing through experimenting with, applying, and measuring consequences. Participants study methods of team action. They measure and evaluate team effectiveness in solving problems with others and experience the measuring of synergy in teamwork. A high point of seminar learning is reached when each participant receives a critique of his or her style of managerial performance from other members of the team. Another is when managers critique the dominant style of their organization's culture, its traditions, precedents, and past practices. A third is when participants consider steps for increasing the effectiveness of the whole organization.

Grid Seminars are intended to aid managers to increase their effectiveness in many different ways. Two approaches are useful in evaluating actual impact on individuals. One is quantitative and involves field research and statistical analysis. The other is qualitative and includes subjective reports.

Quantitative Studies

The following data summarize typical kinds of changes in individual behavior that have been found in field research.[16]

Changes in promotion practices following Grid OD favor merit over seniority.

- Those promoted are three years younger on the average.
- Time of service to promotion is reduced 2.8 years.

■ Promotion rate to higher positions outside plant is up 31%.

Behavior changes are toward sounder relationships.

■ 62% better communication between bosses and subordinates
■ 61% improvement in working with other groups
■ 55% better relationships with colleagues
■ 48% more leveling in one study, 21.8% in another
■ 22% improvement in goal setting
■ 20% more openness to influence
■ 14% increase in delegation

These kinds of changes all are in a more 9,9-oriented direction, and they suggest that significant changes in managerial behavior occur through Grid Seminar participation.

Qualitative Reports

The following comments are typical of participant reactions:

Theories increase understanding and insight.
Now I see a means of improving in a total way rather than a piecemeal way. A sound theoretical framework.

Grid Seminars offer growth-giving personal experiences.
Much greater insight into my managerial style will provide guidelines into how I can improve my effectiveness.

Critique is central to valid problem solving.
Best personal learning experience ever, particularly since individuals and teams learn through experience with continuous critique and positive reinforcements.

Openness is basis to sound relationships.
The frankness and openness created by the Seminar experience is a significant factor in enabling useful discussions to be carried out in depth with team members.

Better teamwork is one of the rewarding outcomes.
I saw synergistic action and understand now that when a group works well together, its end product is superior to

the sum of its products of the same group members
working individually.

*Perspective for seeing one's own performance in more
objective terms.*
It forced me to take a critical look at myself and also,
though practical Grid experience in a team setting,
showed me how some of my beliefs can actually be
detrimental to the company.

Seminar Composition[17]

Although 100% of a firm's managers may be engaged
in organization development, it is rare that all can participate
in Phase 1 Seminars at the same time. Members of a firm
participate in any particular Grid Study team in terms of a
diagonal slice of the membership.

In a diagonal slice Grid team, line and staff managers,
technical and professional personnel, and supervisors study
together. The same is true for personnel of different ages
and organization functions. The only basis for grouping is
that insofar as possible, each Grid team is a representative
sample of the organization. This means that in a diagonal
slice team, several functions of the organization as well as
levels of hierarchy are represented among its members. The
composition is a replica of the company except that no boss
studies with his or her own subordinates (though a boss and
subordinates may attend the same seminar). The diagonal
slice makes possible an exchange of perspective not only
among persons from different functions but among those
from different levels as well.

A frequently expressed reservation about Grid Seminars has to do with whether lower-level members are able
to participate effectively with higher-level ones. The implication is that lower-ranking members, because they are
most likely to be personnel with practical experience, may
not be able to learn as fast as those with college back-
grounds. When learning about behavior, this is not the case.
Lower-level personnel often have a depth of practical experience in human behavior as rich or sometimes even richer
than that of technical personnel. Beyond that, however,

they gain a better understanding of the technical person's thinking—how one goes about analyzing a problem, formulating alternatives, anticipating consequences, and weighing advantages and disadvantages. For a person from the ranks, this is in itself can be an education.

Nonsupervisory personnel are sometimes included in Grid OD, particularly in high technology, knowledge-oriented organizations. Those who engage together in study teams are managers and personnel paid hourly. This is particularly desirable because it permits participants to gain insight into emotions surrounding the cleavage frequently found between the management organization and operating levels. Observers have pointed to this as an important factor in strengthening the effectiveness of lower-level supervisors and improving hourly paid personnel's identification with corporate objectives and their contribution to achievement of those objectives.

Another related question is, "What is the minimum education a person needs to benefit from Grid Seminar participation?" The level of formal education is far less important than the ability to comprehend concepts. Many persons with little formal education have effectively educated themselves. There are limits, but reading comprehension equivalent to the sixth-grade public school level, whether or not the sixth grade was actually completed, usually is essential for learning in a Grid Seminar.

The one disadvantage of diagonal slice selection stems more from the final choice of participants for study teams than from the method itself. It is related to organization level. When levels of participants are too far apart within the hierarchy—vice-president and front-line supervisor in a large company, for example—participants often find it difficulty to interact in an easy and understanding way. While the diagonal slice method is the most desirable of the three, a sound selection of levels should probably be limited to three or four.

Sometimes the question is asked, "Should those who are nearing retirement be included in the development effort?" When a person is nearing retirement, the value in increasing further involvement with the organization is in question. On the other hand, many managers near retirement find gratifying personal reward in the learning itself and in the opportunity to study with others. For these reasons, managers preparing to retire certainly should be invited to participate.

There is no hard-and-fast answer to how many should participate in a seminar, but there are some ground rules. Achieving speed for organization learning and application must be balanced against ensuring that organization performance does not falter because too many people are absent from work at the same time. Under the diagonal slice concept of seminar composition, company after company has found that about ten percent of the organization can be away from the work site without adverse effects on performance. Use of this proportion as a guideline also produces a minimum of disruption of organization teams. The diagonal slice approach ensures that no team is seriously depleted, with the result that those in the seminar can be "covered for" by those on the job.

The ten percent figure ought not to be used automatically in organizations with more than 500 people because it would result in seminars that are too large. The question is, "How many people in an in-house seminar is too many?" The maximum number is around seventy-five for two instructors. Companies with more than 500 managers may send fewer people at any one time, or two seminars (of forty to sixty participants) may be conducted simultaneously but independently.

The stage is set for the first major application to solving work problems after all members of an organization team have attended a Grid Seminar.

Team Building: Phase 2

Team building involves members themselves in diagnosing barriers to sound teamwork and in identifying opportunities for improvement.

Issues of problem solving and decision making—for example, when 1/0, 1/1, and 1/all teamwork are needed—

are central. However, many more facets of teamwork are explored. These include each team member's experience of the contributions of others; the team's culture assumptions about the proper form of teamwork; identification of particular roadblocks that are barriers to effectiveness, with specific plans to remedy them; and, finally, setting team objectives.

Phase 2: Team Building begins when all members of any corporate team have completed Phase 1: Grid Seminar learning and want to apply the concepts to their own managerial team. It starts with the key executive and those who report to him. It then moves down through the organization. Each top-level manager then sits with subordinates as a team and the process is repeated. They study their barriers to effectiveness and plan ways to overcome them.

Team Building Goals

The goals of team building are to

- replace outmoded traditions, precedents, and past practices with a sound team culture;
- set standards for judging excellence;
- increase objectivity in on-the-job behavior;
- use critique for learning; and
- establish objectives for team and individual achievement.

An analysis of the team's culture and operating practices precedes the setting of goals for improvement. Members learn how to become more productive through synergizing their individual contributions. Sound and enduring standards of excellence are identified as benchmarks for the team's use in continually strengthening its problem solving.

Tied into the goal setting for the team is personal goal setting by individual team members. Finally, a demonstration project is selected to enable the team to immediately apply its problem-solving skills to solve a significant, actual barrier to effectiveness with which it is faced.

Grid Team Building is a five-day activity implemented on the job during working hours. If job considerations require it, the activities can be segmented and conducted over a longer period.

Impact on Team Effectiveness

Team building, as indicated in the following quotations, can have major impact on team effectiveness.

> Phase 1 is like getting a check; Phase 2 is when you cash it . . . The period of Phase 2's implementation in the automotive division coincided with a 300% increase in divisional profits—a significantly better profit improvement than that of the rest of the domestic organization—even though we concede that other factors, such as market conditions, expanded plant capacity, the state of the economy, and so on, may have contributed to the improvement in profits. Still, top management believed that Phase 2 and the striking turnaround in the automotive division were more than a coincidence, that Phase 2 made a substantial contribution to the performance picture, even though it was impossible to measure precisely.[18]

> Taken together, Phases 1 and 2 unlock communication barriers between people, among other things.
>
> In the past, when we would set budgets, I would calculate what each department would get. . . . Then they would yell and complain, "Why did you give me this?" I would say, "This is the way it is, boys, I'm the boss." Now, since we went to Grid last year, there's no such happening. Perhaps we've got to reduce our margin in meat. We know we've got to make it up somewhere else. The group comes to a decision. This year it took us an hour-and-a-half to set our budget. Before Grid, we were in there for eight solid hours tablepounding. But now we were committed. . . .
>
> One marketing manager put it this way, "I never realized our department could really work as a team. Phase 1 of the Grid was great, but it really took Phase 2 to bring it all out. Sure, I was apprehensive at first, all the guys were, but when it came right down to it, we were able to work together, solve problems, open up and really communicate with each other. It wasn't what you

would call an easy experience, but it was certainly worthwhile."[19]

The top man of each team retains full responsibility for leadership. Subordinates in the top team then engage in team building in their own teams where *they* are leaders, and this continues throughout the organization.

Intergroup Development: Phase 3

The next step is to achieve better problem solving among groups through closer integration among departments, divisions, or units that have actual working interrelationships. The need for Phase 3 development comes about because while each department, division, or unit has a singular responsibility, each also has overlapping responsibilities. In making decisions, department or division members tend to think more about their singular responsibility and less about the overlap. Because people can see their own immediate interests most clearly, they may act and react more in the interests of their own particular units than in the interests of the entire organization. From inside the department, this is viewed as selflessly serving the corporation. Such preoccupation with a manager's own department means that less attention will be paid to other departments. Then a manager in one department will see those in others as motivated by selfish considerations, particularly when needed cooperation does not seem to be forthcoming. One department may ask, "Why are they dragging their feet? Why are they unable to provide the services we need, which is the only reason for their existence in the first place? They are deliberately disregarding our requirements."

These attitudes are born of frustration and can quickly promote feelings of hostility. A person in Department A may pick up the phone in irritation: "What's the matter with you? Why can't you meet your deadlines? Don't you know how to manage?"

Department B's answer comes back: "Who do you think you are? Remember last week? One of your people miscalculated on a job that forced us into needless overtime and fouled up our schedules, but good!"

Such intergroup hostilities are easily provoked and, once formed, are easily inflamed into win-lose power struggles. Needed cooperation is sacrificed, information is withheld, requests are received as unreasonable demands. When corporate members are asked what their problems are, they tend to answer, "Poor communication between departments." However, the underlying problem of relationships must be dealt with before any fundamental changes in effectiveness of communication can be achieved.

Intergroup Development Goals
The goals of Phase 3 are to

- use a systematic framework for analyzing intergroup coordination problems;
- utilize controlled confrontation to identify focal issues needing resolution to establish integration;
- apply problem-solving and decision-making skills for (a) depolarizing acknowledged antagonisms, (b) confronting relationships based on surface harmony or neutrality that hide problem-solving intergroup difficulties, and (c) resisting compromise when accommodation of differences cannot solve the real problem; and
- plan for achieving improved cooperation between units on a continuing basis.

The beginning activity of intergroup development between any two conflicting groups is devoted to establishing a positive climate and gaining understanding of lack of cooperation, its causes, and barriers to resolution. Establishing objectives, working toward operational improvement, and designing plans for implementation and critique complete the design.

Impact of Intergroup Development
How Phase 3 works in resolving chronic union-management difficulties is described in this quotation.

The union-management Phase 3 has been in progress for eighteen months and has been very successful. The time has been spent systematically analyzing all the important aspects of the union-management relationships. The outcome has been a mutually agreed ideal on each of these aspects plus a whole series of action steps designed to move towards this ideal. Some of the areas covered were overtime, job performance, grievances, seniority, job ownership, the Agreement, work fluctuations, job evaluation, communications, compensation, the pension plan, and objectives.

Overall, these Phase 3 activities have served to develop trust and respect between the union and management participants and have provided an excellent forum for the candid discussion of problems. Many traditions have been broken down and a new culture has emerged. There are two particularly striking features to this new atmosphere. The greatest improvement has come in the area of listening and trying to understand the other side's viewpoint. Secondly, this and the very nature of the Blake operation (management presenting how it sees itself and how it sees the union on various elements, and the union presenting how it sees itself and management) have tended to make both sides more objective. As a consequence, many of the flare-ups that occurred in the early stages are no longer happening.

That is not to say that both sides agree on everything by any means. However, where some disagreement does arise, it is approached rationally and there is a basic trust between the two groups that each is committed to finding a sound and acceptable solution.[19]

As in the example above, Phase 3 is only undertaken by those groups in which actual barriers to effective co-operation exist. It is not a "universal" phase for all members. Intergroup development usually is undertaken after Phase 2: Team Building has been completed.

Designing an Ideal Strategic Organization Model: Phase 4

By the time Phases 1 through 3 have been completed, many outmoded traditions, precedents, and past practices have been replaced by standards of excellence for judging individual performance and effective teamwork and for confronting and resolving conflicts between groups. This is important to corporate excellence, but none of it is sufficient for reaching the degree of excellence potentially available to corporations, based upon systematic development of the business logic being applied throughout an organization for strengthening its bottom-line results.

The key to exploiting organization potentials for excellence to the maximum is in the organization having a clear and explicit business model that defines what it wishes to become in comparison with what it currently is or historically has been.

Goals of Designing an Ideal Strategic Organization Model

The goals of ideal strategic organization modeling are to

- specify minimum and optimum corporate financial objectives;
- describe in explicit terms the nature and character of business activities to be pursued in the future;
- define in operational terms the scope and character of markets to be penetrated;
- create a structure for organizing and integrating business operations for synergistic results;
- delineate basic policies that are to guide future business decision making and operations; and
- identify development requirements for maintaining thrust toward achieving the strategic model and avoiding drag from past ways of doing business.

The model is based on the organization's being engaged in the future in business activity geared to societal needs for products and services; corporation needs for profitability; employee needs for job satisfaction based on involvement, participation, and commitment; and stockholder needs for a meaningful return on invested funds. The top team of a corporation is ideally situated to carry out such a fundamental approach—examining its current practices, rejecting whatever is outmoded and unprofitable, and formulating an ideal strategic replacement model.

Ideal strategic organization modeling is a planning technique that enables the top team to apply rigorous business logic in designing and blueprinting what the organization will become during its next stage of development.

Phase 4 engages the top team in a step-by-step process of business logic study and diagnosis, and in designing its ideal corporate model. The study step is a conceptual investigation of the most basic concepts of business logic that are currently available. These are drawn from, but not limited to, the writings of Alfred P. Sloan, Jr., who pioneered in the development of a systematic discipline of business logic.[20]

Using agreed-upon concepts of "pure" business logic, the next step is to specify the operational properties of a model to serve as a blueprint for corporate reconstruction, led by the top team. Phase 4 is completed when this strategic corporate model has been evaluated and agreed on by senior executives who have a corporate perspective but are not members of the top team and approved by the board of directors as a blueprint for the future.

An example of *actual-ideal* statements developed by one company during its Phase 4 is shown below.

Financial Objectives

Actual	Ideal
Set by president. Based primarily on 10% return on Sales based on return on investment.	Long-range earnings per share growth minimum-double in five years.
15% compounded internal and external growth in sales and earnings/share.	Maintain minimum of 25% return on investment on total assets pretax, based on 5 year moving averages with goal of 33½%.

30% pretax on total assets. Capital gains for shareholders. Growth by reinvestment. Corporate goals not broken down to applicable division objectives.

Reinvest 75% of earnings on 5 year average; corporate goals translated into division goals and planning in specific terms with corporate control to insure achieving them.

Growth financed through: (1) cash flow; (2) debt financing; (3) equity financing test and commitment.

Nature of Business

Actual	Ideal
Manufacture and market high technology electrical equipment and specialized alloys for communication and control.	Survive as an efficient independent organization of human effort.
Growth by acquisition and internal expansion within basic concepts and technological areas.	Diversify and capitalize on common concepts and technological areas to achieve growth objectives.
Maintain "state of art" position.	Develop depth in financial, technological, marketing, R&D, and management within the core group.
Maintain profit to provide for reinvestment.	Common concepts and technological areas to be defined on a business-by-business basis.
Survive with people and profit.	
Core executive group NOT defined.	

Nature of Markets

Actual	Ideal
Limited to U.S. and Canada—some products limited to smaller local areas.	North American based market supplemented by export as justified.
Small number of customers primarily industrial.	Select growth segments of manufacturing markets which we can serve with high quality products.
15–25% significantly affected by national spending (20%).	
High quality market with customers offered a high technology or custom styled product at a high price.	Diversification of markets limited to using technological know-how as a source of synergy (franchise).
Total market available NOT clearly defined.	Enter only those large volume OEM markets wherein our value-added analysis indicates we have a franchise which we can protect.
Significant inhouse potential.	
High gross margin products are marketed.	All things equal, preference will be given to internal sources of supply.
Quality, product service, and delivery.	Division markets differ sufficiently that a separate definition of each to include kinds of customer inventory requirements, and production control will be made and continually updated on an individual basis.

Corporate Structure

Actual	Ideal
Decentralization on a limited basis.	Core management group responsible for corporate policy, and corporate growth, and corporate control.
Components and metals have decentralized production and customer service. Most everything else centralized. Industrial Control—highly decentralized.	Formulation of corporate policy shall be separate from administration of policy.
Central staff and division managers have a dual role and responsibility.	Central staff services act as liaison between divisions to communicate information on new methods and proce-
Two level top team. Financial policy—Top Team. Operating policy—9-man team.	dures and other relevant matters such as application of policy and provide such additional services as are in the best economic interest of
Geography and tradition have influenced degree of decentralization.	the corporation.
Central staff services to metals inadequate in marketing and engineering.	Division managers shall be responsible for production and selling within framework of corporate policy.
Central staff services represent a control problem to components.	Core group shall include the Chief Executive Officer and needs to have deep enough financial, technological,
Management responsibility for corporate growth not properly defined.	marketing, R&D knowledge, and management to make fundamental business decisions without relying on specialized consultation.

$$\underline{\text{CEO}}$$

Core	T and Staff
Group	R&D, En-
	gineering,
	Marketing,
	Personnel

$$\underline{\text{CEO}}$$
Divisions

C/E has responsibility which is unlimited.

Use of Policy

Actual	Ideal
Many policies unwritten, frequently unknown or misunderstood.	Clearly written policy provides objective criteria for managerial action on all elements of corporate activity.
Used for general guidelines with flexibility of interpretation.	Policy provides (defines) direction and long-term growth of the business.
Formulated by at least 3 groups.	Use policy to review corporate performance for the purpose of improving performance as well as improving policy guidelines.
Many policies are traditional.	

Development Requirements

Actual	Ideal
Involving management in building management teams.	Executive talent assessed in terms of meeting and exceeding objective performance criteria.

Use corporate related incentives.

"Throw in and get wet" (sink or swim).

Place talented people in key managerial positions with high autonomy early in their careers to develop competence through on-the-job experience.

Compensation based on performance so that managers have stake in the business and develop an entrepreneurial spirit.

Continue development of a 9,9 culture *throughout the company.*

Impact of Designing an Ideal Strategic Organization Model

The kinds of changes brought about through Phase 4 are described below.

Other important outcomes of the OD effort that must be evaluated are in the area of strategy. Here there is a widespread conviction that the strategic insights that occurred during Phase 4 have been beneficial and have served to start the corporation moving in the right direction.

The Phase 4 team at . . . first reached agreement on details of what actually exists in the present organization model. That is, the team developed a clear picture of . . . management, with no rationalizations, excuses or apologies; they developed simple, concise statements that picture the ideal model today. Then, using the same format, they developed statements as to how a hypothetical ideal . . . would operate. This ideal model served to focus attention on needed changes in policy.

All participants committed themselves to action based on statements of concepts and principles that were agreed upon. In support of these concepts and principles, thirty-nine policies were drafted that are to serve as the specific basis to guide management action.[19]

Implementing Development: Phase 5

The Phase 5 activity moves an organization out of its traditional way of operating and into alignment with the strategic model. Phase 5 is designed so that it is unnecessary to tear down the whole company and start from scratch to build a new company to the requirements of the model. What is done is more like remodeling a building, one room at a time, according to a blueprint of what it is to become. Then architects and engineers study the existing structure to identify what is strong, sound, and consistent with the blueprint and can be retained; what is antiquated and inappropriate to the blueprint and must be replaced; and what is usable but needs modification or strengthening to bring it into line. Once these decisions have been reached, then carpenters, plumbers, and others know what must be done physically to shift from the old to the new. Essentially the same procedure is followed for an organization in which executives and managers design the implementation and either carry it out themselves or involve others at all levels who have the essential know-how to deal with the actual operations subject to concrete change.

Goals of Implementing Development

The goals of Phase 5 are to

- study the existing organization to identify the gaps between how it presently operates and how it is expected to operate, according to the ideal strategic model;
- specify which parts of the business are sound, which parts can be changed and therefore are likely to be retained, which parts are not sound and need to be divested, and new or additional activities that need to be created to meet the requirements of the ideal model;
- design implementation steps to change from the actual to the ideal model; and
- continue to run the business while simultaneously moving it toward the ideal model.

Changing the organization from what it is to what it should be takes place in a series of steps. The first step is analyzing and subdividing the company into its smallest components. The mark of a smallest component is a grouping of interrelated activities that are tied together because they are all essential factors in producing a recognizable source of earnings. The company may be subdivided into many such units.

The next step is to identify all expenses entailed in engaging in these activities. A third step is to compute the investment related to these activities that is tied up in plant, equipment, and so forth. Once these steps have been taken, it becomes possible to evaluate whether or not the business identified by that component meets the business and profit specifications of the ideal strategic corporate model. Test questions such as the following are answered with regard to each of these components.

1. Is the return currently realized on this investment consistent with the profitability objectives of the ideal strategic model?

2. If not, are there controllable expenses, pricing factors, or economics of operation that could be altered to bring it within specified return on investment goals?

3. Is this area of business activity consistent with market areas identified within the ideal strategic model as areas for future penetration and growth?

These test questions are typical of the many employed to decide whether each activity that leads to earnings should be expanded, contracted, changed, or eliminated in pursuing corporate development.

Because of the depth of change involved, the implementation of Phase 5 oftentimes contributes a quantum leap in productivity and profit. The results shown below demonstrate the character of improvement possible.

Impact of Implementing Development

An organization member who was intimately involved in his company's implementation project summarized his reactions.

Once we could specify how we needed to change to meet the ideal strategic model we were in the management-by-objectives business in a way that wasn't limited by blind acceptance of the status quo. Some of the specific things we learned included:

1. How to approach the business in a scientific way to analyze and evaluate variables selectively
2. Taking corporate perspective as opposed to previous functional or departmental view
3. Looking at existing business more critically, growing more and more displeased with current efforts
4. Gaining a new perspective of the role of planning in effective management
5. Focusing on results expected by using return on assets as the basis for business decisions in comparison with conventional profit and loss and share of market thinking
6. Grasping the deeper implications of effective teamwork for increasing the soundness of an implementation plan
7. Developing more basic insight into the dynamics of resistance to change.

Consolidation: Phase 6

Phase 6 is a period used to stabilize and consolidate progress achieved during Phases 1–5 before recycling into another period of change.

Goals of Consolidation

The goals of Phase 6 are to

- critique the change effort to ensure that activities already implemented are continued as planned;
- identify weaknesses that may have appeared throughout the implementation that could not have been anticipated, and take corrective action to rectify them; and
- monitor changes in the business environment (competition, price of raw materials, wage differentials, etc.) that may indicate that fundamental shifts in the model are necessary.

Three features of business life suggest the importance of a consolidating phase in organization development. Managing change is the opposite of managing the tried and true. People tend to repeat the tried and true, but they may lose interest in something that is novel as they become more familiar with it. Reduced effort to make the change work as it was intended may cause it to fail. Phase 6 activities help to identify these drag factors.

A second reason for a period of consolidation is that by continuing study of what is new, additional improvement opportunities may be identified that can add to organizational thrust. A third is that significant alterations in the outer environment may occur that will cause changes specified in the model and implemented in Phase 5 to be more or less favorable than had been anticipated. In either case the monitoring activities of Phase 6 provide a basis for specifying the needs for additional change.

Phase 6 strategies and instruments enable an organization to assess its strengths and consolidate its gains. This is done by organization members' identifying drag factors that may have cropped up and that need to be eliminated to counter their adverse effects. The same is true for thrust factors. These may need to be stressed to gain the full potential of OD.

The significant aspect is making the consolidation phase explicit, rather than assuming that once change has been set in motion, it will persist and gain strength of its own momentum.

When You Are Not the Person in Charge

The introduction of change is a vastly different problem if you are not the person in charge. It may not be within your authority to initiate development, yet you see the importance of bringing sound principles of behavior into organization use. One further assumption is useful in clarifying this problem. Make the assumption that neither *you* nor *your boss* is the person in charge. That means you have no official relationship to those in charge.

How, then, do you proceed to engage the interest and

understanding of others in changing your organization in the direction of applying sound behavioral science principles? Several preliminary steps (summarized on page 181) for getting started constitute possibilities for influencing your boss, who in turn can influence his or her boss, and so on. Eventually awareness is produced at the top.

In addition to being able to further organizationwide development, all individuals are capable of strengthening personal effectiveness with those with whom they associate daily. This is so with their bosses with team members who are colleagues, with other individuals of a similar rank who are associates in other departments, and with subordinates. For example, in the earlier chapter on communications, we described how a 9,9-oriented individual can exercise versatility with respect to asking questions, probing for information, gathering data, and listening. All of these are basic aspects of effectiveness. Many students in the field of managerial effectiveness have concluded that one of the greatest sources of effectiveness is better information. That information is the kind that can only be acquired by gaining direct access to another person on a voluntary and spontaneous basis. A 9,9 orientation is the best way to achieve this access, and communicating in a way that stimulates people to exchange information fully and candidly is an obvious step toward improved effectiveness.

The same kind of generalization applies for working through differences to understanding and agreement by confronting and resolving conflict rather than smoothing, neutralizing, or compromising differences. Every individual has some capacity for keeping a discussion open and fluid and for preventing it from becoming a two-sided win-lose conflict. The secret is to avoid becoming entrapped by another's provocative remarks, simply by keeping one's comments and reactions on a problem-solving plane. In such a situation, the question that a person must answer is, "That was a provocative comment. Should I deal with it in kind and put this person in his or her place, or am I capable of getting the discussion back onto a problem-solving plane by shifting the focus to the issues that are involved?"

A final illustration of what individuals can do within the personal domain of responsibility relates to the use of critique. To see how to do it better the next time, any person who has the will to do so can engage others, even the boss, in postmortem reviews of what happened in a prior cycle of activity. Inviting such a review may expose one to criticism and complaints. However, if the person initiating this effort to use critique in a sound way is capable of withholding impulsive reactions and moving the situation into a critique orientation, there is little or no difficulty in stimulating others to track events in as objective a way as possible and to keep discussion centered upon the learning issue itself rather than on blame assignment. Postmortem critique is a good place to start because it is such a natural thing to do. We do postmortem analyses in everyday living but not necessarily with those who share responsibility for the outcomes under analysis and who could benefit from the conclusions reached. Monday-morning quarterbacking is a postmortem analysis of what went wrong, but the postmortem is not carried out with those who controlled the action. The point is that Monday-morning quarterbacking is an example of the compulsion to analyze critically.

The same is true within the family circle. After children have gone to bed, their parents review their performance and the problems they may be having. This may help one or both parents to relate to the children the next day, but it does little to help the children see the issues that are involved.

In a similar way, husband and wife may discuss their work experiences at home. Reviewing events can help them see the difficulties encountered and why. This is potentially valuable to the learner from the standpoint of how to operate better in the future. The loss is that the people with whom the difficulties were experienced are left out of the critique.

The point is that to critique is a deep human need. The readiness to engage in it is close to the surface. People may not have the requisite skills for doing it without getting emotionally entrapped and becoming either defensive or provocative. But it is this skill of talking about relevant experiences in an objective rather than an emotional way that makes the critical difference between the unproductive use of face-to-face critique and the planned use of it as the basis for maximum learning from experience. On the organizational level it can produce the learning essential for better problem solving.

SUMMARY

Introducing planned change is important because sound principles of behavior only come into use when all individuals who must implement them understand them, appreciate their values, and personally commit themselves to managing in a stronger manner. When sound behavioral science principles become the norms and standards for organizational conduct, maximum contribution to strong management is the result.

It is easiest for the person in charge to introduce change. There are two reasons for this: (1) There is no need to consult superiors for approval, and (2) the financial resources are available for supporting the change process.

There are three ways of introducing change. One is technique-centered OD, which is a mechanical approach. It is little more than announcing a technique, teaching people how to use it, and expecting them to implement it. It disregards two important facts.

The first is that the organization culture may be contradictory to use of the technique. For example, a technique that takes time to apply, such as management-by-objectives, will not be used if managers are under time pressures and therefore have no available time. Operations will come first and management-by-objectives will be disregarded.

The second fact is that every individual approaches the job from the perspective of one or another of the major Grid styles or some combination of them. As a result, a technique-oriented approach, which does nothing to aid an individual to see personal assumptions and learn how to shift from them to stronger principles, simply pulls the technique into the existing Grid style, and applies it accordingly. To a manager who knows nothing about personal

Grid style, 9,9-oriented management-by-objectives becomes 9,1-oriented management-by-objectives.

Process-centered OD is a second possibility. This involves organization members meeting together in their natural groups to study their own behavior and conduct. This is done under the guidance of a change agent who is a catalyst and facilitator. The catalyst works with the needs of the group members as the needs are felt and helps them gather data to explore what can be done to satisfy these needs. As a result, the approach tends to be superficial, and the constructive gains that are achieved when the catalyst is present soon disappear when the facilitator is absent.

The third approach is Grid-centered OD. This involves organization members in learning the theories of the Grid, first in a personal way, with each individual discovering his or her own Grid style in a self-convincing way. Seeing how to shift from characteristic ways of behaving into reliance on behavioral science principles as the basis for working with and through others is the purpose of this learning. Once organization members have learned the Grid and come to see how it relates to them personally, and what they can do to strengthen their effectiveness, these 9,9-oriented principles and values become organization norms and standards. The reinforcing effect of knowing that others are making similar attempts strengthens every person's commitment to increasing personal effectiveness.

Grid-centered development proceeds through a series of phases. By the time it is fully implemented, the nine basic behavioral science principles dealt with here are in place and in daily use.

The problem of introducing change is far different when a person is not in charge. Two possibiities remain. One is to exert upward influence by involving the boss in the basics of Grid-centered development. This can be done through readings, orientation programs, and so on, until awareness is evident at the top. It remains a fact, however, that many individuals interested in introducing change are not able to bring this about.

When an individual is not in charge and is unable to introduce system-oriented change of the sort that deals with the entire organization, many possibilities remain for increasing personal effectiveness. Examples involve better communication, better conflict-solving, and better critique.

The introduction of changes that bring management into line with basic behavioral science principles is basic to the strengthening of individuals and organizations.

14
Is the 9,9 Orientation the Soundest Way for Achieving Results with and Through Others?

T he 9,9 versatility-based orientation and what it entails for effective leadership has been detailed in earlier chapters. Now we turn to the matter of evaluation. Does it make a difference whether or not a person deals with and through others in a 9,9 orientation? What is the evidence?

Limitations in Scholarship and Research

Reductionism is a constant risk in research. It refers to dividing something into the smallest units of behavior possible and designing research to evaluate how those units of behavior shift with changing conditions. The risk of reductionism is that the "whole" behavior is lost sight of, and the research becomes trivial and inconsequential. For example, we know that a boss-subordinate relationship never occurs in a vacuum. It always takes place within the context of a specific organization, which has precedents, rules, and traditions for particular situations—to solve problems, to check progress, to evaluate performance, to critique results, and so forth. Research that examines a boss-subordinate relationship apart from its organizational context is reductionistic and bound to produce spurious results.

Another serious limitation is the failure to separate and distinguish between things that are actually different. Black-white thinking is a good example of this kind of two-sided analysis, and the behavioral sciences are replete with this limitation. McGregor's theories X and Y illustrate the point.[21] Leadership is either X or it is Y. No other possibilities exist; therefore, research at best can conjure only two possibilities, when, in fact, it is evident that two possibilities are too few. Similar limitations are evident in Argyris and Schön's Models I and II.[22] The research of Lewin, Lippett, and White on autocratic, democratic, or laissez-faire styles of leadership is better, but it, too, eliminates important options while putting 9,9 and 5,5 orientations together under the democratic label and the 1,9 and 1,1 orientations together as laissez-faire.[23]

Many behavioral science scholars, investigators, and researchers have fallen into the trap of two-sided thinking. For example, Fiedler's work is limited by two-sided categorization that leaves the most important options out of consideration, yet his research has had significant impact on the field.[24] He conducted research on two kinds of leadership and then concluded that how to lead is contingent on the situation—". . . There is no one best way"! His research design limited the comparison to evaluating the equivalent of only two Grid styles, the 9,1 and 1,9 orientations. He then pointed out that the best leadership style depends on the situation: under certain circumstances the 9,1 orientation works best, in terms of producing results; in others, the 1,9.

The absurdity in this generalization—that there is "no one best way"—is that no data were gathered on the 9,9, the 5,5, or the 1,1 orientations. Only the 9,1 or 1,9 approaches could be evaluated, because all others had been disregarded in the study. Without evaluating the 9,9 approach, his conclusion is certain to be false. Certainly, there is nothing particularly better about 9,1 than 1,9, and in that sense there is "no one best way." Other research has demonstrated that both, however, are inferior to a 9,9 orientation for achieving effective results through people.

Extensive research using the Ohio State instruments to measure leadership effectiveness has produced inconclusive results as to "one best way." [25] In turn, these conclusions have been used to cast doubt on the soundness of a 9,9 orientation. Here again, as with Fiedler's approach, the basic structure of Fleishman's model eliminates 9,9 as an identifiable leadership style. Therefore, summaries of research using this Leadership Behavior Questionnaire and variations of it are irrelevant to evaluating the effectiveness of a 9,9 orientation and comparing it with other leadership styles.

What might be thought of as comparable to the 9,9 orientation in the Fleishman model is referred to as hi-hi. This is actually paternalism in the Grid model. The first hi is created by the boss telling the subordinate on a one-way basis what to do, where and when to do it, and so on. The second hi comes from simultaneously extending a large amount of social-emotional support to the subordinate. This is a coupling of the *production 9* of 9,1 with the *people 9* of 1,9. It combines maximum imposition of direction on the subordinate with maximum social support, and it is strikingly different from a 9,9 orientation.

Still another limitation of research using the Ohio State model is that the system of thinking about the two variables is additive, not interactive. This means you "add" so much of one to so much of the other to get a "score." In the alternative system of thinking, the point at which the two variables interact determines or creates a new kind of behavior, which cannot be predicted simply by adding to so much of the other.

Reflection on 9,9 as contrasted with paternalism shows this difference. A 9 of concern for production coupled with a 9 of concern for people produces a high degree of achievement orientation, but this orientation is in the context of the subordinate's direct involvement and participation in a commitment to designing and implementing the achievement.

Because they are different, an additive theory of leadership and an interactive theory of leadership cannot be superimposed on one another without serious distortions of the kind described here.

Because of these fundamental differences, we see no basis for evaluating the 9,9 orientation as hi-hi on the Ohio State Model, which also provides no clear basis for identifying the 5,5 orientation. Having eliminated the 9,9 and 5,5 orientations, there is no basis for evaluating them.

Thus research predicated either on Fiedler's variables or on the Ohio State dimensions is meaningless relative to the interpretation that there is "no one best way."

Since much research is weakened or rendered invalid by its reductionistic quality or by categorizations that are too coarse, the best solution for evaluating leadership studies is to piece together the evidence from as many sources as possible and try to reconstitute the whole. In some respects this is somewhat like trying to reconstruct a mosaic by considering each piece of the disassembled mosaic separately. Without being able to visualize the whole, each piece that originally fit into the mosaic has lost most of its meaning. Similarly, the pieces of a jigsaw puzzle make little sense without any initial perception of what the picture will look like when the pieces are fitted together properly.

The situation is not quite that bleak, however, since there is such a varied body of scholarship and research from which to construct the whole. Enough of this material overlaps so that parallel conclusions can be obtained from independent sources. Furthermore, the various sources cover such a wide array of populations, situations, and problems that the pattern becomes reasonably clear, once one steps away from each piece to ask, "How does it all fit together?"

Beyond the risks associated with reductionism and categorization, this piecing process itself involves certain hazards. The most important of these is that different researchers have used different research populations and designs, even alternative conceptual formulations of Grid style orientations. These differences make it somewhat risky to treat results from different investigators as if they were comparable and then to put them together. We have used caution to guard against presumptions of equivalence that are not justified, and have combined only those data sources that supplement one another. We have evaluated contradictory and inconsistent results and provide explanations for these where they are appropriate.

The Evidence

Evidence as to the superiority of a 9,9 orientation over other Grid orientations as a basis for working with and through others comes from a wide variety of sources. These include cross-cultural comparisons, cross-scientific disciplines, cross-vocational studies, industrial research on productivity, medical research on physical illness, and research on child rearing.

Cross-Cultural Comparison

Grid Seminars have been conducted under standardized conditions in forty-eight nations of the world, on all continents, and these have provided much comparable data. From these data it is possible to answer the question, "What Grid theory is seen as soundest on a cross-cultural basis?" Knowing what people regard as ideal from the standpoint of soundness is significant. Actions consistent with shared agreement as to what constitutes sound behavior are bound to be more acceptable than those that disregard or run counter to it.

The data were collected in the following manner. After studying Grid theory in prework assignments and during the Seminar,[26] managers engaged in experiments designed to answer the question, "What is the best way for a company to operate?" Twenty specific questions, each dealing with a particular aspect of business behavior and performance, were discussed and deliberated in small study teams, and agreement was reached as to the best answer for each one. The discussion revolved around ranking the five Grid statements, from *5* for the style that they thought represented the soundest down to *1* for the one that was evaluated as the least sound way to run a company. These judgments related to what managers thought to be sound for an effective organization, not necessarily what actually happened in their particular organizations. It should be remembered that these data reflect agreement among managers after they studied the Grid and deliberated the subtleties of each Grid style for approximately thirty hours. Therefore, these judgments can be regarded as quite thorough.

The data for rankings are summarized in Figure 14-1. Any Grid alternative chosen as soundest in all twenty questions received a score of 100. If any particular Grid alternative had been uniformly selected as least sound each time it appeared in the twenty questions, the score would have been 20. These data show that regardless of nation or regional grouping, there is a uniform agreement that the 9,9 orientation is the soundest way to manage a company.[27] This uniformity is demonstrated statistically by the absence of any significant differences among the countries represented. Selected as second best, with about equal frequency, were the 9,1 and 5,5 orientations. The 1,9 orientation was fourth and the 1,1 orientation was regarded as the least sound approach to operating a company. Because these data are from 48 different countries that represent all continents, cut across all major religions, and involve many different languages, the degree of uniformity is striking.

Of course, there might be reservations about these data: "Just because people think it's sound doesn't necessarily mean it is sound*est*." *Perception* of soundest and *empirical demonstration* of soundest are, of course, two different things. However, if the 9,9 orientation were not perceived to be the soundest, the prospect of its empirical use would be nil, as those who manage would resist applying it. We interpret the fact of there being such universal agreement—particularly given the range and variety of reporting populations—to indicate that when people who have actually faced the dilemma of trying to achieve production through others in their daily lives step back from work and look at the options available to them, they uniformly recognize the soundness of 9,9-oriented human productivity relationships. This essentially worldwide agreement is of great potential importance because it demonstrates that there is, even intuitively, a grasp of sound principles of behavior.

FIGURE 14.1
Agreement is present on a cross-cultural basis that the 9,9
orientation is the soundest theory for operating a corporation.

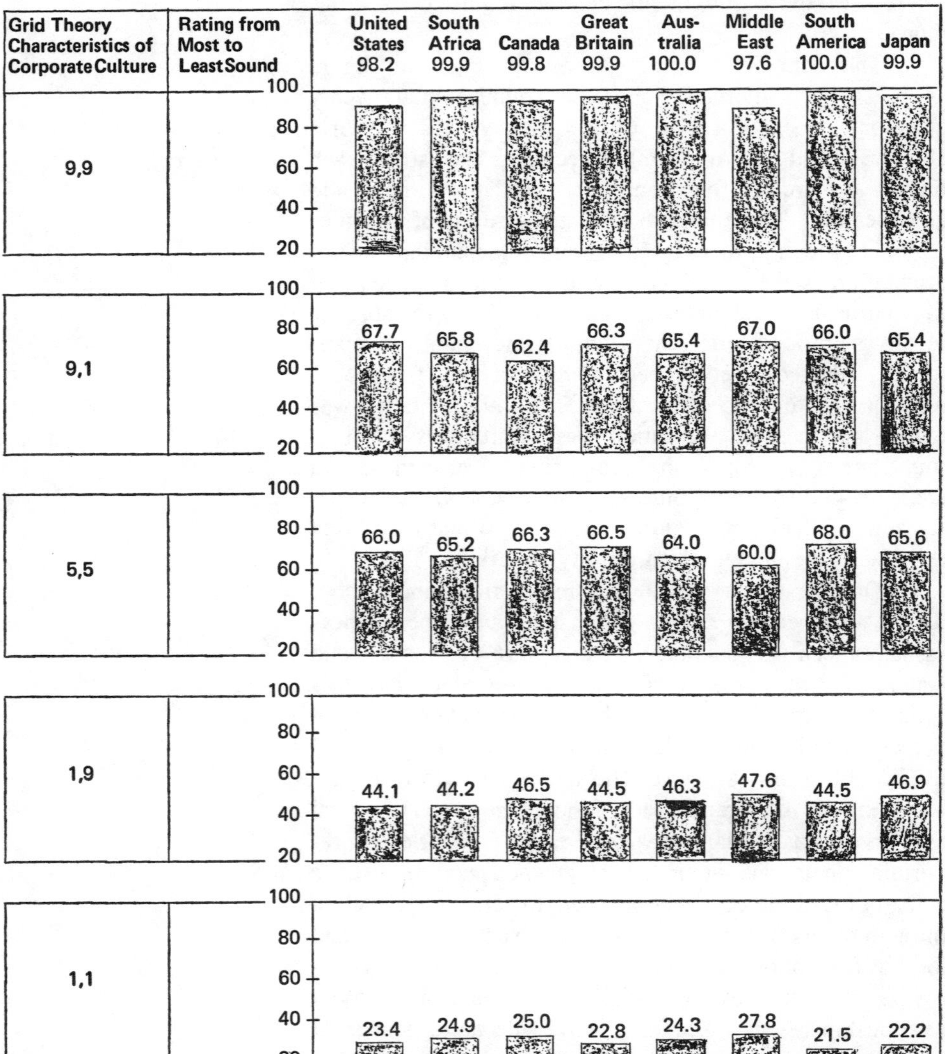

Grid Theory Characteristics of Corporate Culture	Rating from Most to Least Sound	United States 98.2	South Africa 99.9	Canada 99.8	Great Britain 99.9	Australia 100.0	Middle East 97.6	South America 100.0	Japan 99.9
9,9									
9,1		67.7	65.8	62.4	66.3	65.4	67.0	66.0	65.4
5,5		66.0	65.2	66.3	66.5	64.0	60.0	68.0	65.6
1,9		44.1	44.2	46.5	44.5	46.3	47.6	44.5	46.9
1,1		23.4	24.9	25.0	22.8	24.3	27.8	21.5	22.2

Cross-Scientific Disciplines

Another test of the relative value of various Grid styles is made possible by comparing leadership style options as they have been studied and characterized in various disciplines within the behavioral science area. The behavioral sciences incorporate some twenty disciplines. These are areas of scientific investigation of behavior and organization in which efforts are made to identify (1) conditions favorable to effective human behavior and (2) conditions that are likely to produce ineffectiveness.

In these disciplines we find the 9,9 orientation identified as the soundest basis for effectiveness. This repetitive conceptual "discovery" of a 9,9 orientation in discipline after discipline is a source of strong support for the view that there are sound principles of behavior, and that these have been detected and described, regardless of the subject matter of the discipline under examination.

Representative examples may be taken from some of the more popular disciplines. Sociology is a good place to begin. Among the better-known scholars in this field, Thomas and Znaniecki [28] clearly identify three behavioral orientations. They offer an extensive analysis of the 9,9 orientation. The same applies to Durkheim,[29] Etzioni,[30] and Bales.[31]

In the field of psychiatry, psychoanalysis, and clinical psychology, the same trend is evident in an even clearer way. Various Grid orientations have been pictured by almost all major contributors, with a 9,9 description being seen as the soundest from a problem-solving point of view. The following are typical: Berne,[32] Branden,[33] Fromm,[34] Harris,[35] Jung,[36] Maccoby,[37] Missildine and Galton,[38] Wheelis,[39] Heath,[40] Leary,[41] May,[42] Bion,[43] and Horney.[44]. Psychiatrists, psychoanalysts, clinical psychologists, and sociologists see a 9,9 orientation as a sound way of conducting human affairs.

The fields of business management and administration might similarly be commented upon. Here we find presentations picturing a 9,9 orientation in a positive way by Argyris,[45] Burns and Stalker,[46] Follett,[47] Maier,[48] Likert,[49]

McGregor,[50] Lawrence and Lorsch,[51] Moment and Zaleznik,[52] and innumerable others. Comparable demonstrations of the soundness of a 9,9 orientation are available in political science, educational psychology, penology, child psychology, and so on.

Since scholars in any one behavioral science discipline are unlikely to be familiar in depth with other disciplines, this widespread recognition of the 9,9 orientation can be treated as something approaching a series of independent discoveries.

Cross-Vocations

Other sources of evaluation come from studying the soundest Grid orientation in different vocations. Here the Grid framework is used to analyze effectiveness, as it was depicted in an earlier chapter. A series of studies has been written by us, each in collaboration with a person engaged in one particular vocation, to picture how the Grid applies to that particular kind of work. The titles include: *The New Managerial Grid;*[53] *The Grid for Sales Excellence;*[54] *The Real Estate Sales Grid;*[55] *The Grid for Academic Leadership: A Guide for Administrative Excellence;*[56] *The Military Leadership Grid;*[57] *Grid Approaches to Managerial Leadership in Nursing;*[58] and *The Social Worker Grid.*[59]

These sources demonstrate that these vocations are characterized by a variety of relationships, one of which—the 9,9 orientation—experts find to be the soundest and most valid way of achieving effectiveness in outcomes.

Industrial Research on Productivity

Two major sources of research relate a 9,9 orientation to productivity in the industrial context. One of these is work at the Institute of Social Research of the University of Michigan. Likert's research on System 4, which in many respects is the same as a 9,9 orientation, is of both a statistical and a direct experimental intervention nature.[49] The statistical evidence can be interpreted in the following way: "The closer a work group's leadership is to a 9,9 orientation the higher the group's productivity is." This is a conclusion that has been verified over a period of three decades of research involving 50,000 persons working in seventy-five plants or divisions of some twenty-five companies. These results have also been demonstrated in fields such as school systems,[60] hospitals,[61] and voluntary organizations.[62]

The experimental aspect in the Michigan work has involved moving 9,9-oriented managers into low-producing units and evaluating productivity on a before-and-after basis. Results demonstrate that the 9,9-oriented boss brings the section's productivity to a significantly higher level than it had been before the non-9,9-oriented person previously in charge was replaced.[63]

Parallel conclusions are drawn by Argyris and Schön from an in-depth study of six company presidents who changed their behavior from Model I (9,1 orientation) toward Model II (a 9,9 orientation), with concurrent increases in profitability.[64]

The other line of research relates to Grid Organization Development. There are some twenty studies, all of which point to the same conclusion. The most thorough study yet conducted, in which the pitfalls of reductionism were completely avoided,[65] is described hereafter. Figure 14-2 illustrates the profitability of two autonomous corporations operating nationwide on opposite sides of the United States-Canada border. Corporation A engaged in Grid Organization Development. Corporation B did not. They are owned by the same parent, located in a third country. They engage in similar businesses and face the same character of competition in comparable markets.

Starting in 1961, the comparisons show that for five years prior to the introduction of Grid development, the control corporation, B, appeared to be obtaining somewhat better economic performance, but the results were well within the range of chance fluctuations. Then, after introduction of Grid organization development, Corporation A experienced a continuous and rising curve of profitability during the next nine years. By 1974, profitability in the Grid company was 400% greater than in Corporation B, which had not engaged in Grid organization development.

Corporation B had just managed to hold its own over the fourteen-year period.

FIGURE 14.2
Typical Impact of Grid Organization Development

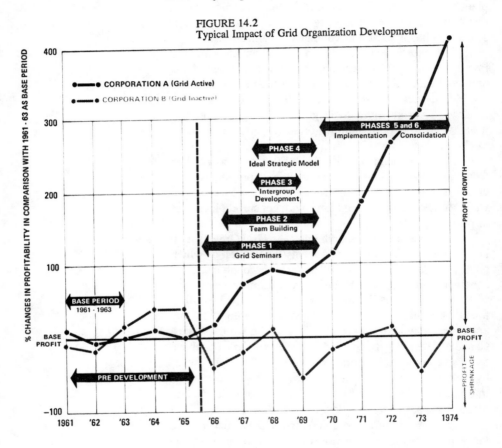

*From "Use of the Grid to Analyze Behavioral Science Approaches to Human Relationships," Blake, Robert R., and Jane S. Mouton. *The New Managerial Grid,* Houston: Gulf Publishing Company, 1978.

The following remarks by the president of Corporation A at a time when his company had been engaged in Grid OD for six years offers his evaluation of the change.

There is no doubt that OD has had a significant and
positive effect on profits . . . . A major objective of the
Grid was to change behavior and values within the
organization in the direction of showing a high concern
for both task accomplishment and human motivation, and
then to sustain these changes and institutionalize them
. . . . There has undoubtedly been a substantial
transformation in this area, with positive effects accruing
through improved communication, the use of critique,
profit or cost consciousness, some aspects of planning,
the handling of conflict, meaningful participation in a
group, and commitment among key managers . . . there
is one other most important benefit that has accrued from
the OD program and that is a substantial improvement in
the working relationships between management and union
officials.

Much of the work involving the union can be
considered as a breakthrough in the application of OD
principles and there is little doubt as to its success.[20]

The model this organization used to change its corporate culture and thus increase profitability is based on six
phases of development described in the previous chapter.
In comparison with studies of organization effectiveness
where a 9,9 orientation is correlated with increased productivity and profitability, there is no study to date demonstrating a positive relationship between situational leadership and increased organization effectiveness.

Other kinds of results that relate Grid style indirectly
to productivity are also of importance. Among the most
important of these are two investigations, both of which
demonstrate that managers with a 9,9 orientation advance
higher on the career ladder than do managers who are oriented to any other Grid style.[66] One of these is based on
a study of 800 managers, another on more than 2000.[67]

Cutting through the differences between one study
and another, the manner in which they have been conducted,
and so on, the evidence available clearly demonstrates that
productivity is enhanced in situations within which 9,9-
oriented principles of sound behavior have been studied and
brought into use.

Some studies report exceptions to the conclusions drawn here about the positive relationship between a 9,9 orientation and productivity. Without analyzing each in detail, Korman provides a summary of them.[68] It can be said that all of them suffer critical design weaknesses in one way or another. One of the most critical of these limitations is that the 9,9 orientation has been excluded from these studies. Another limitation is that often participants have been *told,* in effect, to shift their behavior toward a 9,9 orientation and have been expected to do so without any training or development for gaining the involvement, participation, and commitment of others; for confronting conflict to relieve its causes; or for acquiring the essential synergistic teamwork. In some of these instances positive results have been achieved, but these mean little or nothing, just as no significance can be attached to the failure to achieve positive results. The skills of a 9,9 orientation are not easily gained, and verbal instruction to shift past behavior to new behavior with the expectation of immediate change is totally unrealistic.

Some studies give a modicum of behavioral learning to leaders, who are then expected to modify their own conduct and thereby bring about increased productivity. These experiments have not been very successful because the boss is, in effect, a party to "secrets" about improved ways of behaving that are not known to those who are supervised. Subordinates have known the boss's characteristic behavior for a long time; they have no reason to believe his or her behavior will be any different in the future than it has been in the past. If behavioral changes are noticed, they are likely to be greeted with suspicion and distrust, rather than accepted as demonstrations that increased human resource utilization is in the offing.

The methods of operation cited above significantly limit the effectiveness of a study and offer excellent examples of the effect of reductionism on research. In effect, these interventions in management so completely disregard the variables operating in situations that they ensure failure to demonstrate any positive results. This, however, has nothing to do with evaluating the impact on productivity of operating according to sound principles of behavior.

Medical Research into Physical and Mental Illnesses

The effects of subjective mental states on mental and physical illness have been well established. These subjective mental states are brought about by the circumstances an individual confronts in working with and through others.

Much of this research involves studies of stress. When an individual confronts a focal dilemma for which there is no immediately available solution yet which requires action, the kinds of focal stresses experienced are more intense than those encountered in everyday life. Different focal stresses are related to each of the Grid positions. Thus, there is a focal stress related to the extremes of a 9,1 orientation, with 9,1+ being the desire to control, master, and dominate and 9,1- being fear of failure. The focal stress is created when individuals are striving for domination, control, and mastery, but, regardless of the intensity of effort, success seems never to be realized, at least for more than a fleeting moment. As a result, they put themselves under more and more pressure. Even if they are eventually successful, the satisfactions related to success are short-lived and new heights must be conquered, leading to greater and greater frustration, followed by more and more pressure, and so on, in a vicious circle. It is a known fact that the 9,1 focal stress creates a predisposition to heart attack and other diseases related to the circulatory system.[69] In a similar way, there are clearcut focal stresses related to each of the other major Grid styles *except* the 9,9 orientation.

Let us examine the focal stress related to the extremes of a 1,9 orientation. We have learned that a person operating in a 1,9+ orientation calculates actions to create love and approval. Fear of rejection is the 1,9- motivation.

The focal stress of a 1,9 orientation arises when an individual is compelled to reject others. Medical literature confirms that the focal stress created by frustration of the need to be loved is a predisposing factor in respiratory illness.[70]

Evidence is increasing to show that an extreme 1,1 orientation creates a predisposition to the breakdown of the immunologic system with resultant heightened risk of cancer, tuberculosis, and other diseases.[71,72] An extreme 5,5 orientation, particularly in a turbulent social environment, is a precursor of ulcers and other diseases of the digestive system.[73,74] Extremes of paternalism involve a 9,1-oriented need to dominate, master, and control coupled with a 1,9 need to be loved and approved of. The focal stress often results from a person's curbing outer manifestations of the need for mastery and domination while the internal urge is unrestrained. The urge to dominate is curbed to avoid losing love and approval, a loss that would inevitably result were the tendency to strike out for mastery and domination not suppressed. This way of living and relating to others can be a predisposing circumstance for rheumatoid arthritis.[75]

Many correlations between Grid styles and illness are well documented in medical research and include double-blind studies, in which the behavior was described and predictions of medical outcomes made in advance of the occurrence and diagnosis of actual illnesses. Furthermore, those who diagnosed illnesses had no knowledge of the predictions made at an earlier time. Reports from two centers of this kind of research, The University of Chicago[76] and Johns Hopkins,[77] reach conclusions close enough to one another to be regarded as independent replications.

In addition, much research in the clinical tradition, carried out independently of the Chicago and Maryland studies, reinforces conclusions drawn from these two basic sources.

Only the 9,9 orientation seems to be unrelated to illnesses of various sorts. In fact, the evidence relates a 9,9 orientation to indices of health. It can be interpreted in the following way. A 9,9 orientation is positively related to health, as evidenced in better sleeping and better digestion.[78] Beyond that, people who have learned to deal with others in a 9,9 orientation are more successful in a business or professional sense,[79] have fewer illnesses during the course of their active careers, and may enjoy greater longevity.[80]

Child Rearing

A most crucial test of the 9,9 orientation involves how it is related to successful and unsuccessful ways of child rearing.

Successful child rearing is evident in children who are physically and emotionally healthy, who have a low incidence of problems of delinquency, who are able to enter careers and succeed in them, and who develop enduring marriages rather than become involved in divorce, separation, and so on. These are children who are most likely to be characterized by a 9,9 orientation in adulthood.

The kind of research needed to evaluate these questions is longitudinal in character. While there are some experiments that have the double-blind character mentioned above, there are others where the only possibility of gathering any evidence whatsoever is of the retrospective sort. The researcher knows the outcome and looks to origins for an explanation as to what caused what to happen. This research is less compelling than the double-blind kind. Fortunately, here, too, we find a high degree of correspondence in the conclusions reached, regardless of the circumstances of data gathering.

The first conclusion relating parental Grid style to child rearing is "like-begets-like." The second is that a 9,9 parental orientation is most conducive to mental and physical health of children reared in this way and they, in turn, experience greater success in their marriages and careers. These conclusions are based on tracing the impact of the dominant parent's influence on the child. The dominant parent is the one who ultimately controls the child, particularly in conflict situations. It may be either the mother or the father. When both parents have the same Grid style, there is an additional degree of reinforcement to the like-begets-like conclusion. Other patterns have been identified that create an interesting basis for understanding how child rearing sets the direction of a child's development that may persist through life, though the purpose here is not that of tracking each possible pattern in its detailed sense.

Either of two Grid orientations is produced in the

child by 9,1-oriented parental approaches to child rearing. One is the 9,1 orientation.[81,82] The child who resists the breaking of his or her will and who fights back—seeking to achieve mastery, domination, and control by resisting parents—develops skills of resistance and fighting, and maintains this stance in later life.[83] The other response to a 9,1 parental orientation is the 1,1 orientation, avoidance and withdrawal. Through a "broken" will, the child avoids further pain by minimum exposure of actions that would bring additional criticism.[84]

A dominant 1,9 parental approach to child rearing also is reported to result in a 9,1 orientation in the child.[85] The character of this 9,1 oriented behavior is sometimes stronger or more tyrannical than the behavior of the child whose dominant parent approaches child rearing in a 9,1-oriented way. The 1,9-oriented parent is one who seeks to satisfy the child's every wish and whim. This creates a reaction where the child is more or less completely "spoiled," intolerant of anything of a frustrating quality or any refusal to do his or her bidding. The child makes extreme demands on others, ready to dominate and control by imposing his or her will to get whatever is wanted.

A 1,1-oriented parental situation is found where there is parental neglect, perhaps resulting from environmental pressures on the parent to attend to adult activities. This leads to a 1,1 orientation on the part of the child.[86] It has also been possible to study the 1,1 adult orientation in the child-rearing setting of the orphanage. There is significant evidence that some orphanages are conducted in a sanitary but nonemotional way; that is, they are characterized by a basic 1,1 orientation.[87] These orphanages are undermanned, but the effort is made to keep children clean and fed, even if they are neither stimulated nor loved. Physical needs—cleanliness and feeding—are attended to in a satisfactory way, but the emotional development of the children is affected because of the lack of love.

The 5,5 parental orientation evokes the same orientation in the child. It is a clearcut like-begets-like proposition.[88] When the dominant parent holds before the child the importance of being popular, doing what others do, dressing in ways to earn acceptance, and so on, without stimulating the child through holding out goals to be achieved or standards of excellence, the child learns to do those things that gain popularity and avoid actions that reduce popularity. In many respects, therefore, it is better for a 5,5-oriented youngster to be a C student than an A student, to be a member of the "gang" and get the most common grade, to "run with the crowd."

In none of the above have we seen child-rearing conditions that lead to a child who develops in a 1,9 orientation. A 1,9 orientation does not come about on a like-begets-like basis. There is a reason for this: Paternalism (or maternalism) accounts for children who grow up in a 1,9 orientation.[89] The dominant parent imposes his or her will on the child and then gives the child much love and acceptance in exchange for the child's happy compliance, thus creating a child who does not develop the capacity for independent thought and judgment. Rather, the child comes to look toward adults to know what it is that they want and to fulfill their wishes to gain their love and affection. Thus, the 1,9 orientation in child rearing comes about in quite a different way than any of the other Grid styles.

What about the child-rearing origins of the 9,9 orientation? Here the evidence is that a 9,9 parental orientation produces the same orientation in the child; again, like-begets-like. Parents who respect their children and help in their development through assisting them to explore and experiment within preset limits—who engage with their children in positive and constructive learning experiences— are effectively communicating to the children the importance of openness, of experimenting, of critiquing. The joy that comes from having a close and intimate relationship with another person who is deriving the same emotional satisfactions produces a 9,9 orientation.[90]

IMPLICATIONS
This book has provided an in-depth study of the 9,9 orientation, and a wide range of evidence has been evaluated

to test the proposition that a 9,9 orientation constitutes the most valid basis for dealing with and through others. The subjective logic from personal experience and the evidence from research seems overwhelmingly to support the view that a 9,9 orientation is "best" regardless of the direction one looks. Cross-culture, cross-disciplinary, and cross-vocational research confirms this. Productivity research within the business setting leads to the same conclusion. Adverse effects from extremes of other Grid styles as related to physical illness have been reviewed, and only the 9,9 orientation seems to be associated with good health and longevity. The consequences of parental Grid style for child rearing have been discussed and the conclusion reached that the 9,9 orientation in child rearing is the strongest and best basis for raising healthy children.

Appendix

The original use of the Grid to analyze interactions between significant variables of management—production and people—occurred in our efforts as consultants to understand a basic conflict in a top management group. One faction maintained, "If we don't put the pressure on for higher production, we're going to sink," The other faction said, "We must ease up on the pressure and start treating people in a nicer way." Thus, a 9,1 orientation met a 1,9 orientation. This either-production-*or*-people way of conceiving the problem eliminated perception of other possibilities, such as getting people involved in the importance of being more productive.*

By treating these variables of production and people as independent yet interacting, we came to see many alternative ways of managing: not only 9,1 and 1,9 but also 1,1, 5,5, 9,9, paternalism, counterbalancing, two-hat, statistical 5,5, and facades.

A way of thinking about human relationships that

Grid Study of Behavioral Approaches

*From "Use of the Grid to Analyze Behavioral Science Approaches to Human Relationships," Blake, Robert R., and Jane S. Mouton. *The New Managerial Grid,* Houston: Gulf Publishing Company, 1978.

permitted such clear comprehension and comparison of alternatives led us to believe this formulation to be of general significance for understanding other human relationships. Thus we evaluated in greater detail how others had tried to deal with the subject of human relationships.

We found no systematic use of a two-dimensional geometric space as the foundation for conceptual analysis of assumptions about how to manage, but we were struck by the extent to which such a basis of analysis was being used, either implicitly or statistically. Theorists who used two variables *implicitly*, and without identification of the variables involved, included Horney and Fromm. Other theorists who approached the situation *statistically*, without explicit analysis of how assumptions and therefore behavior may change as a function of the character of the interaction of these variables, included Likert and Fleishman.

The following table, Catalog of Approaches to Human Relationships through a Grid Framework, shows the various implicit or statistical approaches that can be fitted into the Grid. Several explicit efforts to modify the Grid also are included and are commented on.

As shown in the catalog, regardless of their field of specialization, and with but a few exceptions, all investigators describe behavior as if relying on a two-dimensional framework. Factor analytic approaches reinforce conceptual analysis and lead to the conclusion that most meaningful variance in behavior can be accounted for by two factors.

There are exceptions, however. One is Bales, who described behavior in a three-variable geometric space, the third variable being related to an individual's acceptance or rejection of conventional authority. The added complexity did little by way of extending understanding of behavior. Another, by Schutz, added *inclusion* as a third dimension, but inclusion is the motivational scale for the 5,5-oriented theory only. Reddin and Hersey and Blanchard have added *effectiveness* as a third Grid dimension, but this is not a true third dimension since effectiveness is already determined by the first two and therefore is not independent of them. There is an implicit third dimension within the Grid framework, however. It involves identification of motivation as a bipolar scale, ranging—in the 9,1 case, for example—from control, mastery, and domination on the plus end to dread of failure on the minus end of the scale. While adding a third dimension of motivation introduces further clarification as to what a 9,1 orientation is like, little in predictive utility is gained over that already available in a two-dimensional system.

Another concept of importance in understanding the Grid is that of *interaction*. The combination of any two quantities can occur in an arithmetic way. This needs to be distinguished from the fusion of two quantities in a "chemical" way. Hersey and Blanchard, for example, might see 9,9 as a combination of 9 units of task orientation, telling a subordinate in great detail "who, what, where, and how . . ." added to 9 units of relationships, involving extensive compliments and appreciation expressed in response to subordinate compliance. The "chemical" view, by comparison, produces a 9,9 character of interdependence in which shared participation, involvement, and commitment produce consensus-based teamwork. In the former case combination of variables is quantitative and arithmetic; in the latter, it is qualitative and organic; i.e., the *character* of the behavior itself changes, not just the amounts of the behavior.

For the reasons that (1) most investigations have found a two-dimensional basis sufficient and (2) three-dimensional formulations have added little to understanding beyond that already available from the use of two, we conclude that a framework for analyzing behavior that results from two variables is a sound and sufficient basis for comprehending managerial assumptions and practices.

Catalog of Approaches to Human Relationships Through a Grid Framework*

*Reproduced by permission from Robert R. Blake and Jane S. Mouton. *The Grid as a Comprehensive Framework for analyzing Human Relationships* (Austin, Tex.: Scientific Methods, Inc., 1977).

Investigator	Source	Field	9.1	1.9	1.1	5.5	9.9	Statistical 5.5	Facades	Paternalism	Other
Argyris, C.	*Management and Organizational Development: The Path from XA to YB.* New York: McGraw-Hill, 1971.	Organization Behavior	xi, xii, 6-15,66-70,73-74,77-78,85-88,105,107,134,135,138-140			13-14,30-34,56-57	xi, 15-20,21-22,24,42,57-61,67-70,85-89		19	3,62	
Argyris, C. & Schon, D.A.	*Theory in Practice: Increasing Professional Effectiveness.* San Francisco: Jossey-Bass, 1974.	Business Administration	66-84,101-102,104,105-106,107-108,149-155				85-95,101,102-104,105,106-107,108-109				
Arkava, M.L.	*Behavior Modification: A Procedural Guide for Social Workers.* Missoula: U of Montana, 1974	Social Work	16-66					1-11		1-82	
Bach, G.R. & Wyden, P.	*The Intimate Enemy.* New York: William Morrow and Company, Inc., 1969.	Psychology	8-9,45-46,48-49,71-73,75,83,109-117,129,141-150,256-257,311,312,314	5,48,71-73,84-85,97,102-108,311,314,321-322	31-32,312	5,53-54,135-136	36,43,53,91,119-123,137,161-165,257-258,343-348		7,10,13,19,36,103,120,159,196-197,222-223,253-254	113	Sick 9,1 112-113,151,158,160,260 Distorted 1,9,75,112,154,158,160,260,331 Change 173-174

Investigator	Source	Field	9.1	1.9	1.1	5.5	9.9	Statistical 5.5	Facades	Paternalism	Other
Bion, W.R.	*Experiences in Groups.* New York: Basic Books, 1959.	Psychoanalysis	152-153	147-150	152-153	150-152	156-158, 169				Dom/Backup: 160-165
Blake, R.R. & Mouton, J.S.	*The Grid for Sales Excellence: Benchmarks for Effective Salesmanship.* New York: McGraw-Hill, 1970.	Social Psychology	45-58	59-69	70-79	80-94	95-118	187	125-136	188	Dom/Backup: 13-15
Blake, R.R. & Mouton, J.S.	*The Grid for Supervisory Effectiveness.* Austin: Scientific Methods, Inc., 1975.	Social Psychology	11-28	29-43	44-58	59-78	79-107				Dom/Backup: 8-9
Branden, N.	*The Psychology of Self-Esteem.* New York: Bantam Books, 1969.	Psychiatry	188-190	150,151	194-195	185-188	109-139, 146				
Burns, T. & Stalker, G.M.	*The Management of Innovation.* New York: Barnes & Noble, Social Science Paperbacks, 1961.	Organization Behavior	96-125				96-125				
Buzzotta, V.R. Lefton, R.E. Sherberg, M.	*Effective Selling Through Psychology: Dimensional Sales and Sales Management Strategies.* New York: Wiley Interscience, 1972.	Clinical Psychology	36-53, 99-100a, 120-121, 127,264-270,285-286,301-318,319, 320-324, 338-339, 344-347, 357-358, 358-359	68-82, 99-100a, 122,124, 127,274-277,287-288,301-318,319, 340-341, 344-347, 358,359	54-67, 99-100a, 121,122, 127,270-274,286-287,301-318,319, 324,327, 339-340, 344-347, 358,359		83,98, 99-100a, 124,125, 127,199-224,277-283,288-289,301-318,319, 331-334, 341-343, 344-347, 358,359-360		113-117, 291-292		Dom/Backup: 101-112, 289-291

Author	Title	Field									
Durkheim, E.	"On Anomie." In C.W. Mills, ed., *Images of Man: The Classic Tradition in Sociological Thinking.* New York: George Braziller, Inc., 1960, pp. 449-485.	Sociology	455-461	460	460-461	449-461					
Etzioni, A.	*A Comparative Analysis of Complex Organizations.* (Rev. ed.). New York: Free Press, 1975.	Sociology	xxiv.5-6, 8,12,15 27-31,56-59,60-61, 66-67,75-82,84,106 115,116-118,133, 287,455-460,471, 479,486-490,500-504		28,289	xxiv.5-6 6-8,12, 15,40-54, 56-59,61-72,78,81-82,89,92, 106,114-117,169, 305-311, 426-427, 455-460, 471,479 486-490 500-504	471	433-436, 437-438		xxiv,5, 6-8,12, 15,31-39, 62-67,72-75,78-82, 84-87,89, 106,112-113,116, 271,389-391,426-427,455-460,471, 479,486-490,500-504	Machiavellianism: 387
Fleishman, E.A.	"Twenty Years of Consideration and Structure." In E.A. Fleishman and J.G. Hunt, eds., *Current Developments in the Study of Leadership.* Carbondale: Southern Illinois University Press, 1973, pp. 1-40.	Industrial Psychology	25-26, 26-27, 29,32	23,25, 26-27, 29	26-27, 29,32, 36,37	29	23-24, 24-25, 26-27, 27-29, 32,35, 37	37		
Fromm, E.	*The Art of Loving.* London: Unwin Books, 1957.	Psychiatry	23,25, 31,43, 54-55	9,23,25, 42-43, 55-56	15-16, 23,83-84	10-11, 18-22, 25,74-76,80	24,26-28,29, 42,53-54,87, 104-109			82-83

Investigator	Source	Field	9.1	1.9	1.1	5.5	9.9	Statistical 5.5	Facades	Paternalism	Other
Gordon, T.	*Parent Effectiveness Training.* New York: Peter H. Wyden, 1970.	Counseling Psychology	10-11,41-44,83-86, 110,112-113,151, 152,153-159,161, 159,174-183,195, 207,248, 260-261, 263,280, 321-322, 323-324, 325,326-327	11,13-14, 43-44, 151,152, 154-155, 159-161, 184,190-193,248, 251-253, 324-325, 326	44,152, 183,185, 327	42-43, 110,113, 184,289, 322,323, 324,325- 326,327,	12,30-31,33, 47-61, 194-264, 280-282, 305-306	261-263	22-25	11,166, 168-169, 177-178, 190-191	Wide Arc: 11,161-163
Gordon, T.	*T.E.T.: Teacher Effectiveness Training.* New York: Peter H. Wyden, 1974.	Counseling Psychology	27-29,48-49,80-84, 84-85,86-87,184-185,186-189,191, 192-194, 198-206, 211-216	49,85-86, 184,186-188,189-190,191, 206-207	49,87, 206-207, 208-209	208	220-282			194-195, 213	Dom/Backup: 23-24 Wide Arc: 190-191
Hardman, D.G.	*Authority Monograph.* National Council on Crime & Delinquency	Social Work	219,245, 246,248	215-217, 219,249			249-255, 245-254	217,221, 247, 249-255			
Harrington, A.	*The Immortalist.* Millbrae, Calif.: Celestial Arts, 1977.	Philosophy	114,117, 118,119, 123-127, 137,139		117,118, 129-130	100-101, 114-115, 117,118, 127-129	136-139		144-145	120-121	
Harris, T.A.	*I'm OK—You're OK.* New York: Avon, 1969.	Psychiatry	72-73, 263	67-69	69-71, 142-143, 152	143-146, 153	74-77, 151-152, 153,302-304		75-76, 146-151, 152,262-263		

Author	Title	Discipline									Notes
Heath, R.	The Reasonable Adventure: Pittsburgh: The University of Pittsburgh Press, 1964.	Clinical Psychology	ix-x, xii 5-6,20-24,38,39 63-67	28-29		ix,xi,4-5,10-11,14-20,37-38,39,57-63	ix,x,7,8-10,30-36,39	x,xii-xiii,6-7,24-28,38,39,67-69			
Hersey, P. & Blanchard, K.H.	Management and Organizational Behavior: Utilizing Human Resources. (2nd ed.). Englewood Cliffs, N.J.: Prentice-Hall, 1972.	Education	35-37,46-48,61,63,70-76,92-93	61,63,74-76	70-76	74-76	46-48,61,63,70-76	83-86,121-123,127-131		61,63,133-143	Machiavellianism: 92-93 Wide Arc: 125 Change: 149-171
Horney, K.	Neurosis and Human Growth. New York: W.W. Norton & Co., 1950.	Psychoanalysis	17-39,76,97,191-213,214-215,304-306,311-316	76-77,97-98,215-238,239-243,316-324	43-44,77-78,259-290,304,324-328			312-315			Dom/Backup: 232-234 Sick 9.1: 247-256 Distorted 1.9:243-256
Horney, K.	The Neurotic Personality of Our Time. New York: W.W. Norton & Co., 1937.	Psychoanalysis	39,81-82,98,162-187	36,85-87,96-98,102-161	99,191-192,212-213,237	28,96-97	104,107,108,109,113,163,273-274	100-101			Distorted 1.9:259-280
Horney, K.	Self-Analysis. New York: W.W. Norton & Co., 1942.	Psychoanalysis	44,47-48,56-57,57-58,58-59	54-55	48-52,55-56,57,58,59-60,62,108	58,108					Wide Arc: 44
James, M.	The OK Boss. Reading, Mass.: Addison-Wesley, 1975.	Adult Education	10-11,16-17,20-21,35,36,39,40,54,55,56,57,59,61,62,75,76,77,131,139,	13,18-19,37,39-40,75	14-15,35,55,56,57-58,59-61,62,75-76,135,139-140	19,37,77,132,144	17,21,54,55,56,57,59,61,62,69,76-77,132-133,139,144-145,161-163	27,38,64,	106-121,124-127	12-13,35,36,39,73-75	Dom/Backup: 8-9

Investigator	Source	Field	9.1	1.9	1.1	5.5	9.9	Statistical 5.5	Facades	Paternalism	Other
James, M. & Jongeward, D.	*Born To Win: Transactional Analysis with Gestalt Experiments.* Reading, Mass.: Addison-Wesley. 1971.	Education	18,36,68-100,101-126,230	18,37,127-159,230-231	37,50,56-57	18,57-58,58-59,224-226	18,36,56-62,235-238,263-274	2-3,227-228	29-35,58	86,229-230	
Jennings, E.E.	*The Executive: Autocrat, Bureaucrat, Democrat.* New York: Harper & Row, 1962.	Business Education	2,4,20-21,25,66-70,75-77,83-86,86-90,114-163			2,4,90-91,91-97,105-106,164-195,228-232	2-3,4,59-61,97-106,196-234	77-80,256-266	85,250	25-26,149,157-160	Dom/Backup: 117
Jung, C.G.	*Psychological Types.* Princeton: Princeton University Press, 1971.	Psychiatry	346-354,383-387		385-386,388-391,395-398,401-403,403-405	334-335,354-355,356-359,363-366		368-370	384		Dom/Backup: 355-356,362-363,405-407
Kangas, J.A. & Solomon, G.H.	*The Psychology of Strength.* Englewood Cliffs, N.J.: Prentice-Hall, 1975.	Psychology	7-9,10-11,14,15-17,55-56,56-57,135-136	18-19,22,24,78	20-21,21-22,23	11-12,19,57-58	3,9,12,21,23-24,24-25,68-69,117,130-135,136-141,142-145,146-150,151-168	26-27	13-14,17-18,19-20,24-25,29-30,56,77		Wide Arc: 136
Kovar, L.C.	*Faces of the Adolescent Girl.* Englewood Cliffs, N.J.: Prentice-Hall, 1968.	Adolescent Psychology	11-12,73-83,103-106	9-10,53-68	79	10-11,35-51,83,148-149	4-9,107-125,148-149				
Kunkel, F.M. & Dickerson, R.E.	*How Character Develops: A Psychological Interpretation.* New York: Charles Scribner & Sons, 1946.	Psychology	68-81	60-67	80-82		125-140,157-159,176-178				

Author	Title	Category									
Leary, T.	*Interpersonal Diagnosis of Personality.* New York: Ronald Press, 1957.	Clinical Psychology	19,64-65, 104,105, 135,137, 233,269-281,324-331,332-340	64-65, 104,105, 135,233, 292-302, 303-314	19,23-24, 64-65,95-96,104, 105,135, 233,282-291	19,64-65, 135,202-203,233, 315-322	21,64-65, 135,233, 323-324		181-186, 188-191, 282-283, 284-285, 316,317, 318,324, 325,326	64-65, 93	Dom/Backup: 225-227 Distorted 1.9:284-286,288-289,367 Sick 9.1: 341-350, 364,372
Likert, R.	*The Human Organization: Its Management and Value.* New York: McGraw-Hill, 1967.	Organization Behavior	3-12, 13-46			3-12, 13-46	3-12, 13-46, 47-100			3-12, 13-46	
Likert, R. & Likert, J.G.	*New Ways of Managing Conflict.* New York: McGraw-Hill, 1976.	Organization Behavior	19-40, 59-69			19-40	16-17, 19-40, 49-51, 51-56, 71-324			19-40	
McClelland, D.C.	*Power: The Inner Experience.* New York: Irvington Publishers, 1975.	Individual Psychology	7-8,8-12, 13-21,27, 49-51,52-76,77-78, 249,252-254,255-256,257, 258,260-261,264, 266,274-275,295-297,324, 326,328	27,104-122,255, 264,274, 289,322-323,325, 328		27,155, 157-158, 249	27,257, 258,260-261,261-263,263-266,269, 288,301-302,324, 325,329		301-302	35-36, 142-144, 260,289-290	Distorted 1.9:102, 104 Sick 9.1: 255 OD:254, 255
McGregor, D.	*The Human Side of Enterprise.* New York: McGraw-Hill, 1960.	Psychology	33-43				45-57, 61-246				
McGregor, D.	*The Professional Manager.* New York: McGraw-Hill, 1967.	Psychology	59-63, 79-80, 117-118, 118-125, 136-137, 138-140, 148-149	59-63	59-63	59-63, 144-145	29-30, 59-63, 79-80, 118,127-130,130-133,140, 162-182, 191-195			7-10, 142-144	Dom/Backup: 60

Investigator	Source	Field	9.1	1.9	1.1	5.5	9.9	Statistical 5.5	Facades	Paternalism	Other
Maccoby, M.	*The Gamesman.* New York: Simon & Schuster, 1976.	Psychiatry	34,47-48, 76-85, 181-182, 183-184, 187-189, 212-213	183-187	94	34,35, 46-47, 48,50- 75,86- 97,189- 209	179,212, 213-217	100,149	48-49, 91,92- 93,98- 120,121- 171	240-241	
May, R.	*Love and Will.* New York: W.W. Norton & Co., 1969.	Clinical Psychology	45-48, 57-59, 276-278	278-279	27-33	40-45, 279	55-56, 91-92, 146,283- 286,303- 304,306, 310-311				
Meininger, J.	*Success Through Transactional Analysis.* New York: New American Library, 1973.	Business Consultant	26-27, 28-29, 33,39- 40,43- 44,64- 67,73- 75,87- 90,128- 129	29-30, 34-36, 38,43- 44,45- 46,67- 71,75- 76,90- 92,105- 106,166- 170,186- 190	36,39- 40,40- 42,43- 44,56- 57,100- 101,105- 106,110- 113,153, 157	30-31, 57-60, 76-77	26-27, 36-37, 63-64, 101,113- 114,129- 130,158- 160,165- 166,175- 177,178- 185,186- 206	66	7-10,60- 63,78-99, 106-109, 173-175	153, 160-161	Wide Arc: 66 Change: 132-139, 194-204
Metcalf, H.C. & Urwick, L.	*Dynamic Administration: The Collected Papers of Mary Parker Follett.* New York: Harper & Bros., 1940.	Government and Administration	31,50-58, 96-101, 272-277			31-32,35, 210-213, 239	31, 33-49, 58-70, 111-116, 198-202		213-225, 240-246, 260-269, 279-281		

Author	Title	Field	41-67	97-113	123-137	151-169	181-201	80-85	76-80	69-74	Dom/Backup: 15-17
Missildine, W.H.	*Your Inner Child of the Past.* New York: Simon & Schuster, 1963.	Psychiatry	77,85-100,103,106,108-109,125-126,130-133,138-139	77,133-136,157,166,171-191,259-260,266-267,271-272	78-79,101-103,104-105,107-108,109-111,121-124,145-155,156-159,165-166,166-167,243-252,254-259,261						
Missildine, W.H. & Galton, L.	*Your Inner Conflicts—How to Solve Them.* New York: Simon & Schuster, 1974.	Psychiatry	35-36,37,38-39,39-40,62,72-74,76,77,81-82,83-86,131-133,145-146,154-155,171-172,172-180,187-191,196-201,205-207	36,37-38,61,76-77,130	37,39,53-59,60-61,62,62-63,77,120-127,157-160,162-163,184-187		33-34,262-263,308-313				
Moment, D. & Zaleznik, A.	*Role Development and Interpersonal Competence.* Boston: Harvard University Press, 1963.	Business Administration	20,38,56,62-63,67,72,77,80,85-86,87-88,89,104-105,122-123,158-159,160	20,39,56,62-63,67,72,77,78-79,80,83,86-87,89,105-106,123-124,159-160	20,36-37,39,56,62-63,67,72,80,83,87,89-90,106-107,124-125		19-20,36-37,38,41,53,56,62-63,68,72,77,80,85,89,104,120-122				
Mouton, J.S. & Blake, R.R.	*The Marriage Grid* New York: McGraw-Hill, 1971.	Social Psychology									

Investigator	Source	Field	9.1	1.9	1.1	5.5	9.9	Statistical 5.5	Facades	Paternalism	Other
Reddin, W.J.	*Managerial Effectiveness 3-D.* New York: McGraw-Hill, 1970.	Business Administration	27,28-29, 31-32,42, 47,73-74, 94-95, 161,177, 192,194, 194-195, 221-227, 262,263, 268-269	27,28-29, 31,42,68, 73,94, 194,215-219	43,48, 54,194, 209-212, 258-259, 263,264	27,28-29, 30-31,41, 42-43,48, 72-73, 93-94, 194,205-209,213, 231-233	27,28-29,32, 41,48, 74-75, 94,95, 192,194, 230-231, 233-234	52,53-54, 139-140, 149-150, 159-160, 169-178, 181-185, 256-257		42,47	Dom/Backup: 46-47,48, 49,152 Change: 163,307
Reid, W. & Epstein, L.	*Task-Centered Casework.* New York: Columbia U Press, 1972.	Social Work		155-156		136-138	1-260				
Riesman, D., Glazer, N., & Denney, R.	*The Lonely Crowd.* Garden City, N.Y.: Doubleday & Co., 1953.	Sociology Political Science Economic History	23,28-32, 41,57-63		278,281	23,24-28, 33,34-40, 41-42, 63-74, 278	33,278, 282,286-298,328		302-305, 305-307	303	
Roberts, R.W. & Nee, R.H.	*Theories of Social Casework.* Chicago: U of Chicago Press, 1970	Social Work	181-218	33-75, 131-179			77-128, 313-351				
Schutz, W.C.	*The Interpersonal Underworld* (originally titled *FIRO: A Three Dimensional Theory of Interpersonal Behavior).* Palo Alto, Calif.: Science & Behavior Books, 1966.	Psychology	29,41,46, 47-48,89	31,36,41, 47,48,89	25-26, 28-29, 30-31, 41,42, 45-46, 47,48, 89	26-27	27,29-30,31, 37,41, 43,48, 87-89			43	Sick 9.1: 43 Distorted 1.9:42-43

Steiner, C.M.	*Scripts People Live: Transactional Analysis of Life Scripts.* New York: Bantam Books, 1974.	Therapy	53,54-46, 78-81, 115-119, 188-193, 197-198, 231-234, 236-237, 253-261	54,56, 76-78, 198-201, 211-213, 222-224	92-95, 115-119, 178-181, 218-220, 243-245		3,85-86, 352-361, 362-370, 382-383, 384		44-50, 121, 175-178, 304-305	Wide Arc: 39 Dom/Backup: 37-38
Thomas, W.I. & Znaniecki, F.	"Three Types of Personality." In C.W. Mills, ed., *Images of Man: The Classic Tradition in Sociological Thinking.* New York: George Braziller, Inc., 1960, pp. 405-436.	Sociology	427			407-408, 409,411, 418-419, 421,423, 425,427, 428,434, 435-436	408,409, 411,418, 423,435, 436	408-409, 418,423, 433,435, 436	420	
Wheelis, A.	*The Quest for Identity.* New York: W.W. Norton & Co., 1958.	Psychiatry	18,85			18-19, 48-49, 85-89, 91-93, 126	19,20	85		
White, R. & Lippitt, R.	"Leader Behavior and Member Reaction in Three 'Social Climates'." In D. Cartwright and A. Zander, eds., *Group Dynamics: Research and Theory.* (2nd ed.) Evanston, Ill.: Row, Peterson, & Co., 1960, pp. 527-553.	Social Psychology	528-529, 529-532, 537,540-541,541- 546,549-553	528-529, 530,531, 533-534, 539-540, 549-552	528-529, 530,531, 532-538, 539-541, 546-549, 549-553					

References

1.
For further information, see R. R. Blake and J. S. Mouton, *The New Managerial Grid* (Houston: Gulf Publishing Company, 1978); idem, *Making Experience Work: The Grid Approach to Critique* (New York: McGraw-Hill Book Company, 1978); and idem, *Grid Approaches to Managing Stress* (Springfield, Ill.: Charles C Thomas, 1981).

2.
Robert R. Blake and Jane S. Mouton, *Consultation* (Reading, Mass.: Addison-Wesley, 1976), pp. 225–226.

3.
Robert R. Blake and Jane S. Mouton, *Making Experience Work: The Grid Approach to Critique.*

4.
Robert R. Blake and Jane S. Mouton, "Responsibility," in *Improving Productivity Through a 9,9 Versatility Approach to Management* (to be published).

5.
Studs Terkel, *Working* (New York: Random House, 1972).

6.
Eugene Nethvim, "Why Can't Do Nothing Bureaucrats Be Fired?" *The Reader's Digest* 111 (November 1977): 119.

7.
Ibid., p. 120.

8.
Ibid.

9.

Ibid., p. 122.

10.

From the movie production of *Increasing Productivity and Efficiency. Part I: Reviewing Past Efforts* (Postmortem Critique), with Robert R. Blake and Jane Srygley Mouton. Produced by the Bureau of National Affairs, Rockville, Maryland, 1979.

11.

M. Sherif, "A Study of Some Social Factors in Perception," *Arch. Psychol.* 187 (1935).

12.

S. E. Asch, "Studies of Independence and Conformity: I. A Minority of One Against a Unanimous Majority," *Psychological Monograph* 70, no. 9 (1956).

13.

Robert R. Blake and Jane S. Mouton, *Managing Intergroup Conflict in Industry* (Houston: Gulf Publishing Company, 1964).

14.

C. H. Kepner and B. B. Tregoe, *The Rational Manager* (Princeton, N.J.: Kepner-Tregoe, Inc., 1965), pp. 44–51.

15.

Robert R. Blake and Jane S. Mouton, *Corporate Excellence Through Grid Organization Development* (Houston: Gulf Publishing Company, 1968).

16.

Robert R. Blake, Jane S. Mouton, L. B. Barnes, and L. E. Greiner, "Breakthrough in Organization Development," *Harvard Business Review* 42, no. 6 (1964): 133–135.

17.

For a more detailed examination of the rationale underlying seminar composition and administration and the six phases of OD, see Robert R. Blake and Jane S. Mouton, *Corporate Excellence Through Grid Organization Development,* op. cit.

18.

H. A. Hart, "The Grid Appraised—Phases 1 and 2," *Personnel* (September–October 1974): 44–59.

19.

" 'Dialog': A Steinberg Experiment," McGill *Industrial Relations Centre Review* (Fall 1967): 3.

20.

Alfred P. Sloan, Jr., *My Years with General Motors,* edited by

John McDonald with Catherine Stevens (New York: Double-day & Company, Inc., 1972).

21.

D. McGregor, *The Human Side of Enterprise* (New York: McGraw-Hill, 1960), pp. 33–43.

22.

C. Argyris, and D. A. Schön, *Theory in Practice: Increasing Professional Effectiveness* (San Francisco: Jossey-Bass, 1974).

23.

K. Lewin, R. Lippitt, and R. K. White, "Patterns of Aggressive Behavior in Experimentally Created 'Social Climates,' " *Journal of Social Psychology* 10 (1939): 271–299.

24.

F. E. Fiedler, *A Theory of Leadership Effectiveness* (New York: McGraw-Hill, 1967).

25.

A. K. Korman, " 'Consideration,' 'Initiating Structure,' and Organizational Criteria—a Review," *Personnel Psychology: A Journal of Applied Research* 19, no. 4 (1966): 349–361.

26.

J. S. Mouton and R. R. Blake, "OD in the Free World," *Personnel Administration* 32 (1969): 13–23.

27.

B. M. Bass, R. Cooper, and J. A. Haas, *Managing for Accomplishment* (Lexington, Mass.: D. C. Heath and Company, 1970).

28.

W. I. Thomas, and F. Znaniecki, "Three Types of Personality," in C. W. Mills, ed., *Images of Man, the Classic Tradition in Sociological Thinking* (New York: George Braziller, 1960), p. 408.

29.

E. Durkheim, "On Anomie," in C. W. Mills, ed., *Images of Man: The Classic Tradition in Sociological Thinking* (New York: George Braziller, 1960).

30.

A. Etzioni, *A Comparative Analysis of Complex Organizations* (rev. ed.) (New York: Free Press, 1975).

31.

R. F. Bales, *Personality and Interpersonal Behavior* (New York: Holt, Rinehart & Winston, 1970).

32.

E. Berne, *Games People Play* (New York: Grove Press, 1964).

33.

N. Branden, *The Psychology of Self-Esteem* (New York: Bantam Books, 1969).

34.

E. Fromm, *The Art of Loving* (London: Unwin Books, 1957).

35.

T. A. Harris, *I'm OK—You're OK* (New York: Avon, 1969).

36.

C. G. Jung, *Psychological Types* (Princeton: Princeton University Press, 1971).

37.

M. Maccoby, *The Gamesman* (New York: Simon & Schuster, 1976).

38.

W. H. Missildine and L. Galton, *Your Inner Conflicts—How to Solve Them* (New York: Simon & Schuster, 1974).

39.

A. Wheelis, *The Quest for Identity* (New York: W. W. Norton & Co., 1958).

40.

R. Heath, *The Reasonable Adventurer* (Pittsburgh: The University of Pittsburgh Press, 1964).

41.

T. Leary, *Interpersonal Diagnosis of Personality* (New York: Ronald Press, 1957).

42.

R. May, *Love and Will* (New York: W. W. Norton & Co., 1969).

43.

W. R. Bion, *Experiences in Groups* (New York: Basic Books, 1959).

44.

K. Horney, *Neurosis and Human Growth* (New York: W. W. Norton & Co., 1950); *The Neurotic Personality of Our Time* (New York: W. W. Norton & Co., 1937); *Self-Analysis* (New York: W. W. Norton & Co., 1942).

45.

C. Argyris, *Management and Organizational Development: The Path from XA to YB* (New York: McGraw-Hill, 1971).

46.
T. Burns and G. M. Stalker, *The Management of Innovation* (New York: Barnes & Noble, Social Science Paperbacks, 1961).

47.
M. P. Follett, *Dynamic Administration: The Collected Papers of Mary Parker Follett* (New York: Harper & Bros., 1940).

48.
N. R. F. Maier, *Problem-Solving Discussions and Conferences: Leadership Methods and Skills* (New York: McGraw-Hill, 1963).

49.
R. Likert, *The Human Organization: Its Management and Value* (New York: McGraw-Hill, 1967).

50.
D. McGregor, *The Professional Manager* (New York: McGraw-Hill, 1967).

51.
P. Lawrence and J. Lorsch, *Organization and Environment: Managing Integration and Differentiation* (Boston: Harvard University School of Business Administration, Division of Research, 1967).

52.
D. Moment and A. Zaleznik, *Role Development and Interpersonal Competence* (Boston: Harvard University Press, 1963).

53.
R. R. Blake and J. S. Mouton, *The New Managerial Grid* (Houston: Gulf Publishing Co., 1978).

54.
Idem, *The Grid for Sales Excellence* (2d ed.) (New York: McGraw-Hill Book Company, 1980).

55.
Idem, *The Real Estate Sales Grid* (Englewood Cliffs, N.J.: Prentice-Hall, Inc., 1980).

56.
Idem, *The Grid for Academic Leadership: A Guide for Administrative Excellence* (San Francisco, Calif.: Jossey-Bass, 1981).

57.
Idem, *The Military Leadership Grid* (in press).

58.
R. R. Blake, J. S. Mouton, and M. Tapper, *Grid Approaches*

to Managerial Leadership in Nursing (St. Louis, Mo.: C. V. Mosby, 1980).

59.
R. R. Blake, J. S. Mouton, L. Tomaino, and S. Gutierrez, *The Social Worker Grid* (Springfield, Ill.: Charles C Thomas, 1979).

60.
B. Cullers, C. Hughes, and T. McGreal, "Administrative Behavior and Student Dissatisfaction: A Possible Relationship," *Peabody Journal of Education* (Jan. 1973), 155–163; F. Feitler and A. Blumberg, "Changing the Organization Character of a School," *The Elementary School Journal* (January 1971), 206–215.

61.
B. S. Georgopoulos and F. C. Mann, *The Community General Hospital* (New York: Macmillan, 1962); B. S. Georgopoulos and A. Matejko, "The American General Hospital as a Complex Social System," *Health Service Research* 2, no. 1 (Spring 1967): 76–112.

62.
A. S. Tannenbaum, *A Study of the League of Women Voters of the United States: Factors in League Effectiveness* (Ann Arbor: University of Michigan Institute for Social Research, 1958); A. S. Tannenbaum, and M. N. Donald, *A Study of the League of Women Voters of the United States: Factors in League Functioning* (Ann Arbor: University of Michigan Institute for Social Research, 1957).

63.
R. G. Likert and J. G. Likert, *New Ways of Managing Conflict* (New York: McGraw-Hill, 1976).

64.
C. Argyris and D. A. Schön, *Increasing Leadership Effectiveness* (New York: John Wiley & Sons, 1976), pp. 183–210.

65.
R. R. Blake, and J. S. Mouton, *The New Managerial Grid.*

66.
Ibid., pp. 204–205.

67.
J. Hall, "To Achieve or Not: The Manager's Choice," *California Management Review* 18, no. 4 (1976), 5–18.

68.
A. K. Korman, " 'Consideration' . . . —a Review."

69.

M. Friedman and R. H. Roseman, *Type A Behavior and Your Heart* (Greenwich, Conn.: Fawcett Crest, 1974).

70.

Several clinical investigations and controlled experiments confirm the close association reported. See F. Alexander, *Psychosomatic Medicine: Its Principles and Applications* (New York: W. W. Norton & Co., 1950); R. Fine, "The Personality of the Asthmatic Child," in H. I. Schneer, ed., *The Asthmatic Child* (New York: Hoeber, 1963); I. D. Harris, et al., "Observations on Asthmatic Children," *American Journal of Orthopsychiatry* 20 (1950): 490; L. Jessner, et al., "Emotional Impact of Nearness and Separation for the Asthmatic Child and His Mother," *Psychoanalytic Study of the Child* 10 (1955): 353; and L. Rees, "The Importance of Psychological, Allergic, and Infective Factors in Childhood Asthma," *Journal of Psychosomatic Research* 7 (1964): 253.

71.

L. LeShan, *You Can Fight for Your Life* (New York: M. Evans & Co., 1977), pp. 64–66.

72.

This point of view is formulated in G. W. Kisker, *The Disorganized Personality* (2d ed.) (New York: McGraw-Hill, 1972), p. 295; F. Dunbar, *Mind and Body: Psychosomatic Medicine* (New York: Random House, 1950), pp. 233–239; and G. F. Derner, *Aspects of the Psychology of Tuberculosis* (New York: Hoeber, 1953).

73.

Evidence from sociologic and anthropologic studies indicates that people who get into and conform with the norms of the group in which they hold membership seem to have lower levels of susceptibility to disease, particularly when the environment is homogeneous and undemanding. See L. E. Hinkle, Jr., and H. G. Wolff, "An Investigation of the Relation Between Life Experience, Personality Characteristics, and General Susceptibility to Illness," *Psychosomatic Medicine* 20 (1958): 278–295; D. C. Leighton, et al., *The Character of Danger*, vol. 3 (New York: Basic Books, 1963); J. T. Cassel, "Physical Illness in Response to Stress," in S. Levine and N. A. Scotch, eds., *Social Stress* (Chicago: Aldine, 1970), pp. 189–209. Hinkle, Leighton, and Cassel all state that people conforming to culturally acceptable patterns tend to be mentally and physically more healthy. See also G. E. Moss, *Illness, Immunity, and Social Interaction* (New York: John Wiley & Sons, 1973), p. 155. Moss also suggests that those who become alienated from their membership group are more susceptible to disease than those who hold membership. See Moss, pp. 170–172.

74.
The role of anxiety in peptic ulcer context is clarified by G. F. Mahl and R. Karpe, "Emotions and Hydrochloric Acid Secretion During Psychoanalytic Hours," *Psychosomatic Medicine* 15 (1953): 312.

75.
H. R. Weiner, *Psychobiology and Human Disease* (New York: Elsevier, 1977). See also J. W. Mason, "A Re-Evaluation of the Concept of 'Non-Specificity' in Stress Theory," *Journal of Psychiatric Research*, vol. 8, nos. 3 and 4 (August 1971): 323–333.

76.
F. Alexander, T. M. French, and G. H. Pollock, *Psychosomatic Specificity* (Chicago: University of Chicago Press, 1968); G. H. Pollock, "The Psychosomatic Specificity Concept," *The Annual of Psychoanalysis* 5 (1977): pp. 141–168.

77.
C. B. Thomas and K. R. Duszynski, "Closeness to Parents and the Family Constellation in a Prospective Study of Five Disease States: Suicides, Mental Illness, Malignant Tumor, Hypertension, and Coronary Heart Disease," *The Johns Hopkins Medical Journal* 134, 5 (May 1974): pp. 251– 270.

78.
A. H. Maslow, *Motivation and Personality* (New York: Harper, 1970), pp. 156, 159, 161, 166–168.

79.
H. Levinson, "How Good Is Your Mental Health?" *Reader's Digest* (September, 1965): 54–58.

80.
H. Selye, *Stress Without Distress* (Philadelphia: J. B. Lippincott Company, 1974).

81.
E. L. Koos, *Families in Trouble* (Morningside Heights, N.Y.: King's Crown Press, 1946), pp. 37–38.

82.
A view of how the power orientations of society are related to child rearing and how these, in turn, influence adult patterns

of adjustment is provided in D. Riesman, N. Glazer, and R. Denny, *The Lonely Crowd* (Garden City, N.J.: Doubleday, 1950), pp. 59–63; and G. D. Bell, *The Achievers* (Chapel Hill, N.C.: Preston-Hill, 1973), pp. 24–27.

The more 9,1 the assumptions of parents regarding child rearing, the greater likelihood that, because of their own needs, they compel their children to work, to save, to clean house, to study, and so on, all to prove themselves "acceptable." See M. R. Winterbottom, "The Relation of Childhood Training in Independence to Achievement Motivation," in J. W. Atkinson, ed., *Motives in Fantasy, Action, and Society* (Princeton: D. Van Nostrand, 1958), pp. 453–478; and L. W. Hoffman, S. Rosen, and R. Lippitt, "Parental Coerciveness, Child Autonomy, and Child's Role at School," *Sociometry* 26 (1960): 15–22.

One of the richest analyses of parental influences on children and how these, in turn, emerge as adult styles is by K. Horney, *The Neurotic Personality of Our Time*, p. 170. How parents stimulate a child's motivation to dread failure is discussed by Missildine and Galton, *Your Inner Conflicts*, pp. 196–201. Parent behavior may become a model to the child for how he should treat others. This is discussed by K. Horney, *The Neurotic Personality of Our Time*, p. 87.

83.

There is general agreement that punitive 9,1-oriented parents produce hostile and aggressive children who can also be punitive on a "like-begets-like" basis. See W. H. Missildine, *Your Inner Child of the Past* (New York: Simon & Schuster, 1963), pp. 204–209; Missildine and Galton, *Your Inner Conflicts*, pp. 38–39; and G. D. Bell, *The Achievers*, pp. 41–43.

84.

Unpredictable parental behavior may result in 1,1 withdrawal by the child. See K. Horney, *The Neurotic Personality of Our Time* (New York: W. W. Norton & Co., 1937), p. 275; and Bell, *The Achievers*, pp. 61–62. Reliance on severe punishment as a parental basis of child rearing is described in Missildine, *Your Inner Child of the Past*, pp. 121–122; and Missildine and Galton, *Your Inner Conflicts*, pp. 120–121.

85.

With 1,9-oriented parents children learn to be demanding to gain from parents what they wish. In this manner they learn 9,1-oriented skills. See A. Adler, *Social Interest: A Challenge to*

Mankind (New York: Capricorn Books, 1964), p. 149; Horney, *The Neurotic Personality of Our Time,* p. 87; and Missildine, *Your Inner Child of the Past,* p. 132. See also R. H. Blum, *Horatio Alger's Children, The Role of the Family in the Origin and Prevention of Drug Risk* (San Francisco: Jossey-Bass, Inc., Publishers, 1972), p. 54.

86.
Parental neglect resulting from environmental pressures on the parent for adult activities is described by Missildine in *Your Inner Child of the Past,* pp. 231–233. Withdrawal, indifference, and uninvolvement is a childhood reaction to parental neglect. See N. Branden, *The Disowned Self* (New York: Bantam, 1971), pp. 7–9.

87.
Institutional neglect and its impact upon the emotional and intellectual development of the child is described in H. L. Bakwin, "Loneliness in Infants," *American Journal of Diseases of Children* 63 (1942): 30; R. A. Spitz, "Hospitalism," in O. Fenichel, ed., *The Psychoanalytic Study of the Child* (New York: International University Press, 1945); W. Goldfarb, "Effects of Early Institutional Care on Personality, Behavior," *Child Development* 14 (1943): 213; Missildine, *Your Inner Child of the Past,* pp. 234–235, 243; Missildine and Galton, *Your Inner Conflicts,* pp. 184–187; and J. Bowlby, "Some Pathological Processes Set in Train by Early Mother-Child Separation," *Journal of Mental Science* 99 (1953): 265–272.

88.
R. H. Blum, *Horatio Alger's Children,* p. 55; and E. L. Koos, *Families in Trouble,* p. 37.

89.
How paternalistic control is exercised over a child is documented in L. C. Kovar, *Faces of the Adolescent Girl* (Englewood Cliffs, N.J.: Prentice-Hall, 1968), pp. 53–56, 62–63. Parents who overcontrol a child are likely to develop dependency in him. Thus, autonomy and the capacity for self-direction have little or no opportunity to develop. Evidence is presented in H. Fensterheim and J. Baer, *Don't Say Yes When You Want to Say No* (New York: Dell, 1975), p. 27; P. Wylie, *Generation of Vipers* (New York: Pocket Books, Inc., 1955), pp. 197–198; and Bell, *The Achievers,* pp. 74–75. Horney also comments on how a child's confidence can be undermined.

See K. Horney, *The Neurotic Personality of Our Time*, pp. 85–86.

90.

Kovar, *Faces of the Adolescent Girl*, pp. 4–5, 6–7, 107–111. Riesman, Glazer, and Denney *The Lonely Crowd*, pp. 328; F. M. Kunkel and R. E. Dickerson, *How Character Develops: A Psychological Interpretation* (New York: Charles Scribner & Sons, 1946), pp. 125–140, 157–159, 176–178; Bell, *The Achievers*, pp. 104–105; M. D. S. Ainsworth and B. A. Witting, "Attachment and Exploratory Behavior of One-Year-Olds in a Strange Situation," in B. M. Foss, ed., *Determinants of Infant Behavior*, vol. 4 (1969): pp. 111–136; E. Douvan and J. Adelson, *The Adolescent Experience* (New York: Wiley, 1966); R. Dreikurs and L. Grey, *Logical Consequences: A New Approach to Discipline* (New York: Meredith Press, 1968), pp. 62–82; W. A. Westley and N. B. Epstein, *The Silent Majority* (San Francisco: Jossey-Bass, Inc., Publishers, 1969), pp. 165–166; Adler, *Social Interest*, p. 29; R. Dreikurs, R. Corsini, and S. Gould, *How to Stop Fighting with Your Kids* (Chicago: Ace Printing, 1974), pp. 49–56; J. D. Campbell and M. R. Yarrow, "Perceptual and Behavioral Correlates of Social Effectiveness," *Sociometry* 24 (1961): 1–20; A. H. Maslow, "Creativity in Self-Actualizing People," in H. H. Anderson, ed., *Creativity and Its Cultivation* (New York: Harper, 1959), pp. 85–86, 88; H. S. Sullivan, *The Interpersonal Theory of Psychiatry* (New York: Norton, 1953); and M. R. Yarrow, P. M. Scott, and C. Z. Waxler, "Learning Concern for Others," *Developmental Psychology* 8 (1973): 240–260.

Index